Economics of
Petroleum Reservoirs

By

Roshdy Ebrahim, Ph.D

Roshdy Ebrahim

Copyright © 2018 Roshdy Ebrahim

All right reserved

ISBN: 9781980772286

Preface

The 1850s saw the beginnings of the global petroleum industry. The raw material ('rock oil') was known, thanks to seepages in a number of places, and the decline of whaling (due to the scarcity of whales), which led to increased interest in alternatives for lighting purposes. These discoveries were prompted by the introduction of distilled coal oil (Young, 1850–1851) and kerosene (1853). Interest was further stimulated by Benjamin Silliman's pioneering work on fractional distillation of petroleum (1855), and the rising price of liquid fuels such as kerosene (due to the scarcity of whale oil) for household illumination. It was Silliman's report to an investor group, that later became the Pennsylvania Rock Oil Company, that kicked off the search for petroleum in western Pennsylvania.

Oil and gas resources have provided much of the world's energy in the twentieth century and are expected to be an important part of the energy mix well into the twenty-first century. Currently, oil and gas provide approximately 63 % of primary energy consumption in Europe. However, energy security in the region remains a concern.

The concern is reinforced due to Europe's dependence on oil and gas from other regions. In addition, many commentators fear domestic oil and gas resource depletion will produce significant supply scarcities in the short term, i.e., well before 2020. Thus, the purpose of this analysis is to address the subject by estimating conventional and unconventional oil and gas supply cost curves for the region.

The implementation of carbon capture and storage (CCS) at extraction sites could also increase cost, though presumably the cost would be lower than that resulting from the imposition of emissions penalties. Meanwhile, enhanced oil and gas recovery based on CO2 injection would be potentially less expensive due to emissions offsets based on sequestered CO2.

The geologic structure in which petroleum has been trapped and has accumulated, whether it was the source rock or the rock to which petroleum has migrated, is called the petroleum reservoir.

In summary, the formation of a petroleum reservoir involves first the accumulation of the remains of land and sea life and their burial in the mud and sedimentary materials of ancient seas. This is followed by the decomposition of these remains under conditions that recombine the hydrogen and carbon to form the petroleum mixtures. Finally, the formed petroleum is either trapped within the porous source rock when a cap rock exists or it migrates from the source rock to another capped (sealed) structure.

Contents

Preface 3

Contents 6

Introduction 10

1. Types of Petroleum Reservoirs 24
   1.1. Geologic Classification of Petroleum Reservoirs 24
   1.2. Reservoir Drive Mechanisms 28
   1.3. Reservoir structures 31

2. Reservoir Rocks 41
   2.1. Porosity of Reservoir Rocks 44
   2.2. Petrography 55
      2.2.1. Pre-microscopic Observations 56
      2.2.2. Microscopic Observations 57
   2.3. Permeability of Reservoir Rocks 61
   2.4. Compressibility of Reservoir Rocks . 63
   2.5. Sensitivity of Reservoir Rocks 65
   2.6. Assessment Methods of Reservoir Sensitivity 66
   2.7. Types of Reservoir Space 67
   2.8. Buried Depth and Compaction 69
   2.9. Fluid Saturation of Reservoir Rocks 71
   2.10. Critical gas saturation 83

3. **Fossil Energy Reserves**............................89
   3.1. Oil Reservoir 97
      3.1.1. Classifying Oil Reserves 104
      3.1.2. Volatile Oil Reservoir.............113
      3.1.3. Black Oil Reservoir.................114
      3.1.4. Heavy Oil Reservoir 117
      3.1.5. CRUDE CONDITIONING AND STORAGE 118
      3.1.6. Tar Sand 121
      3.1.7. Distribution of Unconventional Crude Oils 124
   3.2. Gas Reservoir..................................126
      3.2.1. Smart Methods......................142
      3.2.2. Dry Gas Reservoir 151
      3.2.3. Wet Gas Reservoir 154
      3.2.4. Gas condensate 161
      3.2.5. Tight Gas Reservoirs 163
      3.2.6. Unconventional Gas 166
4. Separation of Natural Gas from Crude Oil 172
5. Estimated Volumes of Remaining Oil and Gas Resources..173
6. Oil recovery 179

6.1. Principles of Enhanced Oil Recovery 179

6.1.1. ESTIMATION OF INITIAL OIL IN PLACE BY THE MATERIAL BALANCE METHOD FOR A SOLUTION GAS DRIVE RESERVOIR 189

6.1.2. OIL IN PLACE AND RECOVERABLE RESERVE BY THE VOLUMETRIC METHOD 189

6.1.3. DISPERSED GAS INJECTION PERFORMANCE 195

6.1.4. Hydrocarbon Recovery and Treatment 196

6.1.5. FUTURE RESERVOIR PERFORMANCE 198

6.1.6. POLYMER FLOOD PERFORMANCE 198

6.1.7. Chemical Recovery 199

6.1.8. Miscible Recovery 201

6.1.9. Thermal Recovery 201

6.1.10. Pressure Maintenance 203

6.1.11. Water Flooding 204

6.2. Intensification and Reversal of the Oil Recovery 205

6.3. Improved Petroleum Recovery 207

6.4. Major differences between oil and gas field development 208

6.5. Enhance shale resources 211

7. CONVENTIONAL PETROLEUM 232

7.1. Reserves–Production Ratio 233

7.2. Reservoir Management.................235

7.3. Economic Balance in Oil Fields (Optimization) 236

8. Peak Oil: How Long Can We Depend on Oil and Other Fossil Fuels? 241

8.1. Economic Impacts of Peak Oil and Decreasing EROI 252

9. Oil reservoirs in some countries 263

9.1. Nigeria..263

9.2. Angola...265

9.3. Ghana..268

9.4. china...270

References 273

Biography of the author..............................277

introduction

Predictions of future shortages of oil began shortly after commercial production started in the late nineteenth century. In the first half of the twentieth century, there was national concern about imminent and irreversible shortages of oil on at least six occasions. In the 1950s M. King Hubbert, a geophysicist at Shell Development Company in Houston, developed a model of a cycle of production of finite nonrenewable resources that aimed to predict future production from analysis of production-to-date and estimates of the amount of remaining resource in the ground. In a series of publications Hubbert predicted that US oil production would peak by 1975 at the latest: actual peak production was in 1970. The peak in US production gave credence to Hubbert's methodology, which is now commonly referred to as the "Hubbert curve.

Fears arose of global depletion of fossil energy resources. In 1972 a report for the Club of Rome, a global think tank, examined known reserves of oil and gas and predicted the time of total depletion under various scenarios. Assuming exponential growth in consumption, the report predicted depletion of known reserves of oil by 1992 and natural gas by 1994. Even under what was considered an optimistic scenario wherein reserves could be increased fivefold by new exploration, oil was predicted to be totally depleted by 2022 and gas by 2021. These predictions, though influential at the time, proved unfounded largely because consumption did not increase at an exponential rate.

In 1962 Hubbert predicted that world oil production would peak in 2000 and, again, in 1969 predicted the peak would be between 1990 and 2000. As the turning point of the millennium approached predictions of "peak oil" increased. Most of the predictions suggested a peak in the first years of the twenty-first century. For example, in 1988 Campbell, using the Hubbert curve analysis, predicted a peak between 2000 and 2005. Actual production between 2006 and 2010 has been 4.7% higher than in the previous 5 years. However, predictions of imminent "peak oil" persist and proponents point out that production has been relatively level for the last 6 years (to 2010). Others point to global political and economic reasons for the recent relatively flat production rate.

The basic problem with the Hubbert curve analysis is that estimates of remaining resources change through time. The amount of oil and gas on the planet is undoubtedly finite. The amount is large but much of it would be prohibitively expensive to produce using present-day technologies. Resource estimates therefore tend to focus on oil and gas accumulations that are anticipated to be economically viable for production, either at present or within the foreseeable future. Advances in technology, however, may make accumulations technically accessible at lower costs over time, thus increasing the size of estimated remaining resources. In addition, advances in geologic concepts and subsurface imaging through geophysical techniques have shown oil and gas resources to be substantially more extensive than was at one time thought. As a result, many predictions using the Hubbert curve analysis have been far less successful than Hubbert's prediction of US peak production. Hubbert in 1962, for example, predicted US natural gas production would peak in 1975 but production in 2010 was at an all-time high.

Another example is Campbell's 1988 prediction that underestimated US oil production in 2010 by 70%. [1]

in order to meet the resources needs for national economy modernization and sustainable development, it is necessary that [2]

(a) find out new oil and gas reservoirs to increase resources backup reserves;

---

[1] Ripudaman Malhotra: Fossil Energy. Springer Science+Business Media New York 2013. P 10: 11
[2] Xuetao Hu • Shuyong Hu Fayang Jin • Su Huang: Physics of petroleum Reservoirs, Petroleum Industry Press, Beijing, China 2017. P 2

(b) apply advanced technologies to maximize the reasonable development of hydrocarbon reservoirs;

(c) enhance the recovery of existing oil and gas fields to increase petroleum production;

(d) develop international cooperation and participate in the development of international oil and gas resources, to satisfy the requirement of national petroleum industry in exploiting domestic and international resources facing domestic and international markets;

(e) utilize adequately various energy-saving measures, alternative energy, and new energy to reduce the pressure in petroleum demand.

The definitions that are used to describe petroleum reserves are often misunderstood because they are not adequately defined at the time of use. Therefore, as a means of alleviating this problem, it is pertinent at this point to consider the definitions used to describe the amount of petroleum that remains in subterranean reservoirs.

Petroleum is a resource; in particular, petroleum is a fossil fuel resource. A resource is the entire commodity that exists in the sediments and strata, whereas the reserves represent that fraction of a commodity that can be recovered economically. However, the use of the term reserves as being descriptive of the resource is subject to much speculation. In fact, it is subject to word variations. For example, reserves are classed as proved, unproved, probable, possible, and undiscovered.

Proven reserves are those reserves of petroleum that are actually found by drilling operations and are recoverable by means of current technology. They have a high degree of accuracy and are frequently updated as the recovery operation proceeds. They may be updated by means of reservoir characteristics, such as production data, pressure transient analysis, and reservoir modeling.

Probable reserves are those reserves of petroleum that are nearly certain but about which a slight doubt exists. Possible reserves are those reserves of petroleum with an even greater degree of uncertainty about recovery but about which there is some information. An additional term potential reserves is also used on occasion; these reserves are based on geological information about the types of sediments where such resources are likely to occur and they are considered to represent an educated guess. Then, there are the so-called undiscovered reserves, which are little more than figments of the imagination. The terms undiscovered reserves or undiscovered resources should be used with caution, especially when applied as a means of estimating reserves of petroleum reserves. The data are very speculative and are regarded by many energy scientists as having little value other than unbridled optimism.

The term inferred reserves is also commonly used in addition to, or in place of, potential reserves. Inferred reserves are regarded as of a higher degree of accuracy than potential reserves, and the term is applied to those reserves that are estimated using an improved understanding of reservoir frameworks. The term also usually includes those reserves that can be recovered by further development of recovery technologies.

The differences between the data obtained from these various estimates can be considerable, but it must be remembered that any data about the reserves of petroleum (and, for that matter, about any other fuel or mineral resource) will always be open to questions about the degree of certainty. Thus, in reality, and in spite of the use of self-righteous word-smithing, proven reserves may be a very small part of the total hypothetical or speculative amounts of a resource.

At some time in the future, certain resources m ay become reserves. Such a reclassification can arise as a result of improvements in recovery techniques which may either make the resource accessible or bring about a lowering of the recovery costs and render winning of the resource an economical proposition. In addition, other uses may also be found f or a commodity, and the increased demand may result in an increase in price. Alternatively, a large de posit may be come exhausted and unable to produce any more of the resource, thus forcing production to focus on a resource that is lower grade but has a higher recovery cost.

It is very rare that petroleum (the exception being tar sand de posits, from which most of the volatile material has disappeared over time) does not occur without an accompanying cover of gas. It is therefore important, when describing reserves of petroleum, to also acknowledge the occurrence, properties, and character of the gaseous material, more commonly known as natural gas.

More recently, the Society for Petroleum Engineers has developed a resource classification system that moves away from systems in which all quantities of petroleum that are estimated to be initially- in-place are used. Some users consider only the estimated recoverable portion to constitute a resource. In these definitions, the quantities estimated to be initially- in-place are (1) total petroleum-initially-in-place, (2) discovered petroleum-initially-in- place, and (3) undiscovered petroleum-initially-in-place. The recover able portions of petroleum are defined separately as (1) reserves, (2) contingent resources, and (3) prospective resources. In any case and whatever the definition, reserves are a subset of resources and are those quantities of petroleum that are discovered (i.e., in known accumulations), recover able, commercial and remaining.

The total petroleum- initially-in-place is that quantity of petroleum that is estimated to exist origin ally in naturally occurring accumulations. The total petroleum-initially-in-place is, therefore, that quantity of petroleum that is estimated, on a given date, to be contained in known accumulations, plus those quantities already produced there from, plus those estimated quantities in accumulations yet to be discovered. The total petroleum-initially-in-place may be subdivided into discovered petroleum-initially-in-place and undiscovered petroleum-initially in- place, with discovered petroleum-initially-in -place being limited to known accumulations.

It is recognized that the quantity of petroleum-initially-in-place may constitute potentially recover able resources since the estimation of the proportion that may be recover able can be subject to significant uncertainty and will change with variations in commercial circumstances, technological developments and data availability. A portion of those quantities classified as unrecoverable may become recoverable resources in the future as commercial circumstances change, technological developments occur, or additional data are acquired.

Discovered petroleum-initially-in-place is that quantity of petroleum that is estimated, on a given date, to be contained in known accumulations, plus those quantities already produced therefrom. Discovered petroleum-initially-in-place may be subdivided into commercial and sub commercial categories, with the estimated potentially recoverable portion being classified as reserves and contingent resources respectively (as defined below).

Estimated recoverable quantities from known accumulations that do not fulfill the requirement of commerciality should be classified as contingent resources. The definition of commerciality for an accumulation will vary according to local conditions and circumstances and is left to the discretion of the country or company concerned. However, reserves must still be categorized according to specific criteria and, therefore, proved reserves will be limited to those quantities that are commercial under current economic conditions,

	Production		
	Reserves		
Proved	Proved plus probable	Proved plus probable plus possible
	Contingent resources		
Low estimate	Best estimate	High estimate
	Unrecoverable		
	Prospective resources		
Low estimate	Best estimate	High estimate
	Unrecoverable		

← Range of uncertainty →

Not to scale

whereas probable and possible reserves may be based on future economic conditions. In general, quantities should not be classified as reserves unless there is an expectation that the accumulation will be developed and placed on production within a reasonable timeframe.

In certain circumstances, reserves may be assigned even though development may not occur for some time. An example of this would be where fields are dedicated to a long-term supply contract and will only be developed as and when they are required to satisfy that contract.

Contingent resources are those quantities of petroleum that are estimated, on a given date, to be potentially recoverable from known accumulations, but which are not currently considered as commercially recoverable. Some ambiguity may exist between the definitions of contingent resources and unproved reserves. This is a reflection of variations in current industry practice, but if the degree of commitment is not such that the accumulation is expected to be developed and placed on production within a reasonable timeframe, the estimated recover able volumes for the accumulation may be classified as contingent resources. Contingent resources may include, for example, accumulations for which there is currently no viable market, or where commercial recover y is de pendent on the development of new technology, or where evaluation of the accumulation is still at an early stage.

Undiscovered petroleum-initially-in -place is that quantity of petroleum that is estimated, on a given date, to be contained in accumulations yet to be discovered. The estimated potentially recover able portion of undiscovered petroleum-initially-in -place is classified as prospective resources, which are those quantities of petroleum that are estimated, on a given date, to be potentially recover able from undiscovered accumulations.

Estimated ultimate recover y (EUR) is the quantity of petroleum which is estimated, on a given date, to be potentially recover able from an accumulation, plus those quantities already produced therefrom. Estimated ultimate recover y is not a resource category but it is a term that may be app lied to an individual accumulation of any stat us =maturity (discovered or undiscovered).

Petroleum quantities classified as reserves, contingent resources or prospective resources should not be aggregated with each other without due consideration of the significant differences in the criteria associated with their classification. In particular, there may be a significant risk that accumulations containing Contingent Resources or Prospective

Resources will not achieve commercial production.

The range of uncertainty reflects a reasonable range of estimated potentially recoverable volumes for an individual accumulation. Any estimation of resource quantities for an accumulation is subject to both technical and commercial uncertainties, and should, in general, be quoted as a range. In the case of reserves, and where appropriate, this range of uncertainty can be reflected in estimates for proved reserves (1P), proved plus probable reserves (2P) and proved plus probable plus possible reserves (3P) scenarios. For other resource categories, the terms low estimate, best estimate, and high estimate are recommended.

The term best estimate is used as a generic expression for the estimate considered the closest to the quantity that will actually be recovered from the accumulation between the date of the estimate and the time of abandonment. If probabilistic methods are used, this term would generally be a measure of central tendency of the uncertainty distribution. The terms low estimate and high estimate should provide a reasonable assessment of the range of uncertainty in the best estimate.

For undiscovered accumulations (prospective resources) the range will, in general, be substantially greater than the ranges for discovered accumulations. In all cases, however, the actual range will be dependent on the amount and quality of data (both technical and commercial) that is available for that accumulation. As more data become available for a specific accumulation (e.g., additional wells, reservoir performance data) the range of uncertainty in the estimated ultimate recovery for that accumulation should be reduced.

The low estimate, best estimate, and high estimate of potentially recoverable volumes should reflect some comparability with the reserves categories of proved reserves, proved plus probable reserves, and proved plus probable plus possible reserves, respectively.

Although there may be a significant risk that sub commercial or undiscovered accumulations will not achieve commercial production, it is useful to consider the range of potentially recoverable volumes independently of such a risk. [1]

---

[1]James G. Speight: The Chemistry and Technology of Petroleum. FOURTH EDITION. Taylor & Francis Group, LLC. 2007. P 104:107

1. Types of Petroleum Reservoirs

Petroleum reservoirs are generally classified according to their geologic structure and their production (drive) mechanism.

1.1. Geologic Classification of Petroleum Reservoirs

Petroleum reservoirs exist in many different sizes and shapes of geologic structures. It is usually convenient to classify the reservoirs according to the conditions of their formation as follows.

Dome-shaped and anticline reservoirs—These reservoirs are formed by the folding of the rock layers as shown in Figure. The dome is circular in outline, and the anticline is long and narrow. Oil or gas moved or migrated upward through the porous strata where it was trapped by the sealing cap rock and the shape of the structure.

Faulted reservoirs—These reservoirs are formed by shearing and offsetting of the strata (faulting), as shown in Figure. The movement of the nonporous rock opposite the porous formation containing the oil/gas creates the sealing. The tilt of the petroleum-bearing rock and the faulting trap the oil/gas in the reservoir.

Salt-dome reservoirs—This type of reservoir structure, which takes the shape of a dome, was formed due to the upward movement of a large, impermeable salt dome that deformed and lifted the overlying layers of rock. As shown in Figure 1.3, petroleum is trapped between the cap rock and an underlying impermeable rock layer, or between two impermeable layers of rock and the salt dome.

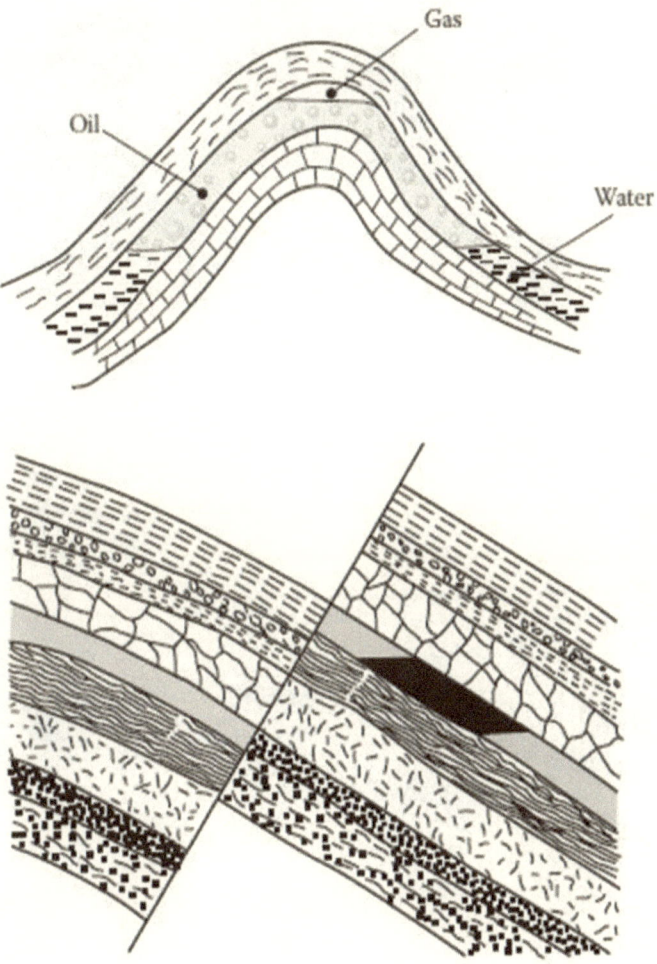

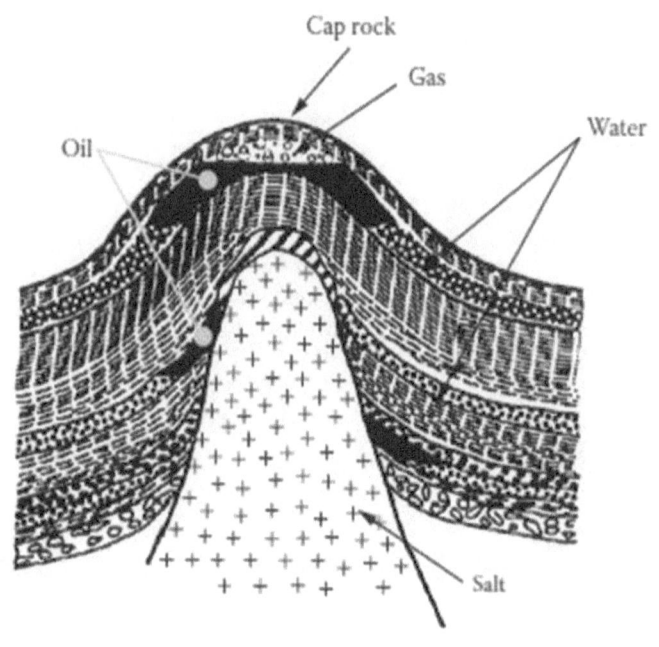

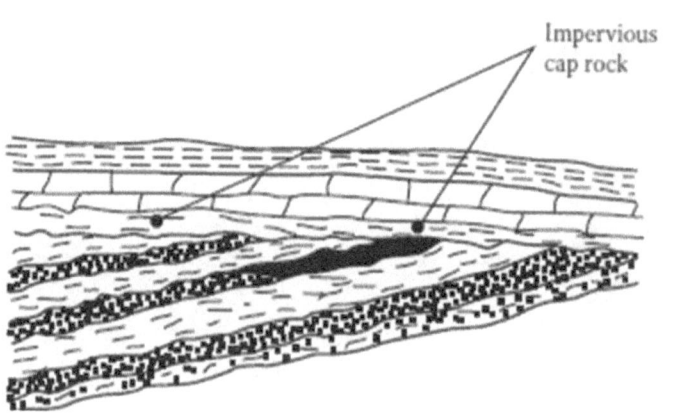

Unconformities—This type of reservoir structure, shown in Figure, was formed as a result of an unconformity where the impermeable cap rock was laid down across the cutoff surfaces of the lower beds.

Lense-type reservoirs—In this type of reservoir, the petroleum-bearing porous formation is sealed by the surrounding, nonporous formation. Irregular deposition of sediments and shale at the time the formation was laid down is the probable cause for this abrupt change in formation porosity.

Combination reservoirs—In this case, combinations of folding, faulting, abrupt changes in porosity, or other conditions create the trap from this common type of reservoir. [1]

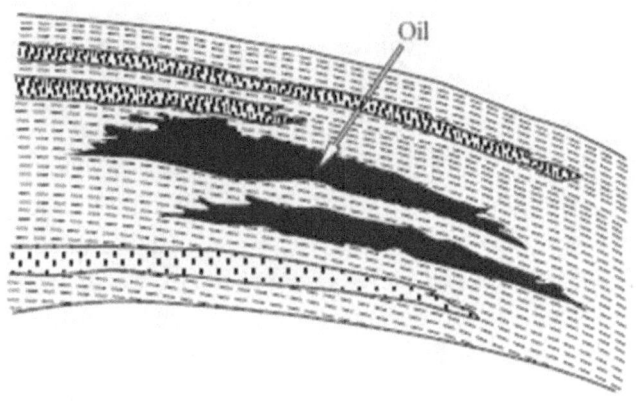

[1] Hussein K. Abdel-Aal Mohamed A. Aggour Mohamed A. Fahim: Petroleum and Gas Field Processing. Second Edition. Taylor & Francis Group, LLC. 2016. P 9: 11

1.2. Reservoir Drive Mechanisms

At the time oil was forming and accumulating in the reservoir, the pressure energy of the associated gas and water was also stored. When a well is drilled through the reservoir and the pressure in the well is made to be lower than the pressure in the oil formation, it is that energy of the gas, or the water, or both that would displace the oil from the formation into the well and lift it up to the surface. Therefore, another way of classifying petroleum reservoirs, which is of interest to reservoir and production engineers, is to characterize the reservoir according to the production (drive) mechanism responsible for displacing the oil from the formation into the wellbore and up to the surface. There are three main drive mechanisms:

1. Solution gas drive reservoirs—Depending on the reservoir pressure and temperature, the oil in the reservoir would have varying amounts of gas dissolved within the oil (solution gas). Solution gas would evolve out of the oil only if the pressure is lowered below a certain value, known as the bubble point pressure, which is a property of the oil. When a well is drilled through the reservoir and the pressure conditions are controlled to create a pressure that is lower than the bubble point pressure, the liberated gas expands and drives the oil out of the formation and assists in lifting it to the surface. Reservoirs

with the energy of the escaping and expanding dissolved gas as the only source of energy are called solution gas drive reservoirs. This drive mechanism is the least effective of all drive mechanisms; it generally yields recoveries between 15% and 25% of the oil in the reservoir.

2. Gas cap drive reservoirs—Many reservoirs have free gas existing as a gas cap above the oil. The formation of this gas cap is due to the presence of a larger amount of gas than can be dissolved in the oil at the pressure and temperature of the reservoir. The excess gas is segregated by gravity to occupy the top portion of the reservoir.

In such reservoirs, the oil is produced by the expansion of the gas in the gas cap, which pushes the oil downward and fills the pore spaces formerly occupied by the produced oil. In most cases, however, solution gas is also contributing to the drive of the oil out of the formation. Under favorable conditions, some of the solution gas may move upward into the gas cap and, thus, enlarge the gas cap and conserves its energy. Reservoirs produced by the expansion of the gas cap are known as gas cap drive reservoirs. This drive is more efficient than the solution gas drive and could yield recoveries between 25% and 50% of the original oil in the reservoir.

3. Water drive reservoirs—Many other reservoirs exist as huge, continuous, porous formations with the oil/gas occupying only a small portion of the formation. In such cases, the vast formation below the oil/gas is saturated with salt water at very high pressure. When oil/gas is produced by lowering the pressure in the well opposite the petroleum formation, the salt water expands and moves upward, pushing the oil/gas out of the formation and occupying the pore spaces vacated by the produced oil/gas. The movement of the water to displace the oil/gas retards the decline in oil, or gas pressure, and conserves the expansive energy of the hydrocarbons.

Reservoirs produced by the expansion and movement of the salt water below the oil/gas are known as water drive reservoirs. This is the most efficient drive mechanism; it could yield recoveries up to 50% of the original oil. [1]

1.3. Reservoir structures

the earth's crust is part of a dynamic system and movements within the crust are partly accommodated by rock deformation. Like any other material, rocks may react to stress with an elastic, ductile or brittle response, as described in the stress–strain diagram in Figure.

---

[1]Hussein K. Abdel-Aal Mohamed A. Aggour Mohamed A. Fahim: Petroleum and Gas Field Processing. Second Edition. Taylor & Francis Group, LLC. 2016. P 12: 13

It is rare to be able to observe elastic deformations (which occur for instance during earthquakes) since by definition an elastic deformation does not leave any record. However, many subsurface or surface features are related to the other

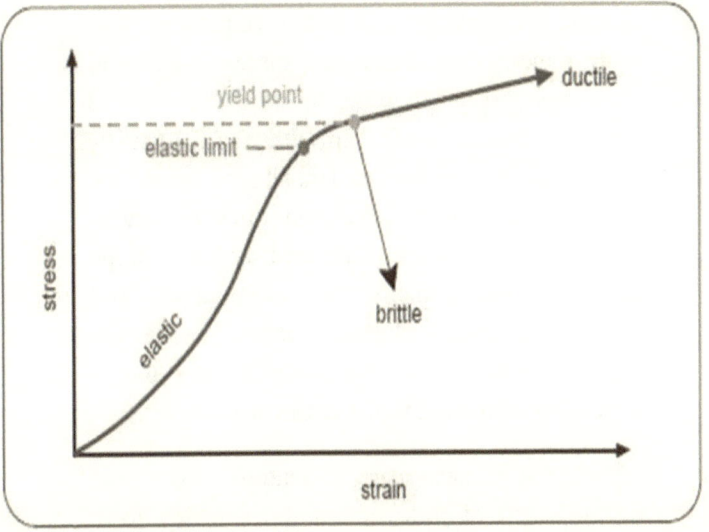

two modes of deformation. The composition of the material, confining pressure, rate of deformation and temperature determine which type of deformation will be initiated.

If a rock is sufficiently stressed, the yield point will eventually be reached. If a brittle failure is initiated, a plane of failure will develop which we describe as a fault. The Figure shows the terminology used to describe normal, reverse and wrench faults.

Since faults are zones of inherent weakness they may be reactivated over geologic time. Usually, faulting occurs well after the sediments have been deposited. An exception to this is a growth fault (also termed a syn-sedimentary fault). They are extensional structures and can frequently be observed on seismic sections through deltaic sequences. The fault plane is curved and in a three-dimensional view has the shape of a spoon. This type of plane is called listric. Growth faults can be visualized as submarine landslides caused by rapid deposition of large quantities of water-saturated sediments and subsequent slope failure. The process is continuous and concurrent with sediment supply, hence the sediment thickness on the downthrown block is expanded compared to the upthrown block.

A secondary feature is the development of rollover anticlines which form as a result of the downward movement close to the fault plane which decreases with increasing distance from the plane. Rollover anticlines may trap considerable amounts of hydrocarbons.

Growth faulted deltaic areas are highly prospective since they comprise thick sections of good-quality reservoir sands. Deltas usually overlay organic-rich marine clays which can source the structures on maturation. Examples are the Niger, Baram or Mississippi Deltas. Clays, deposited within deltaic sequences may restrict the water expulsion during the rapid sedimentation/compaction. This can lead to the generation of overpressures.

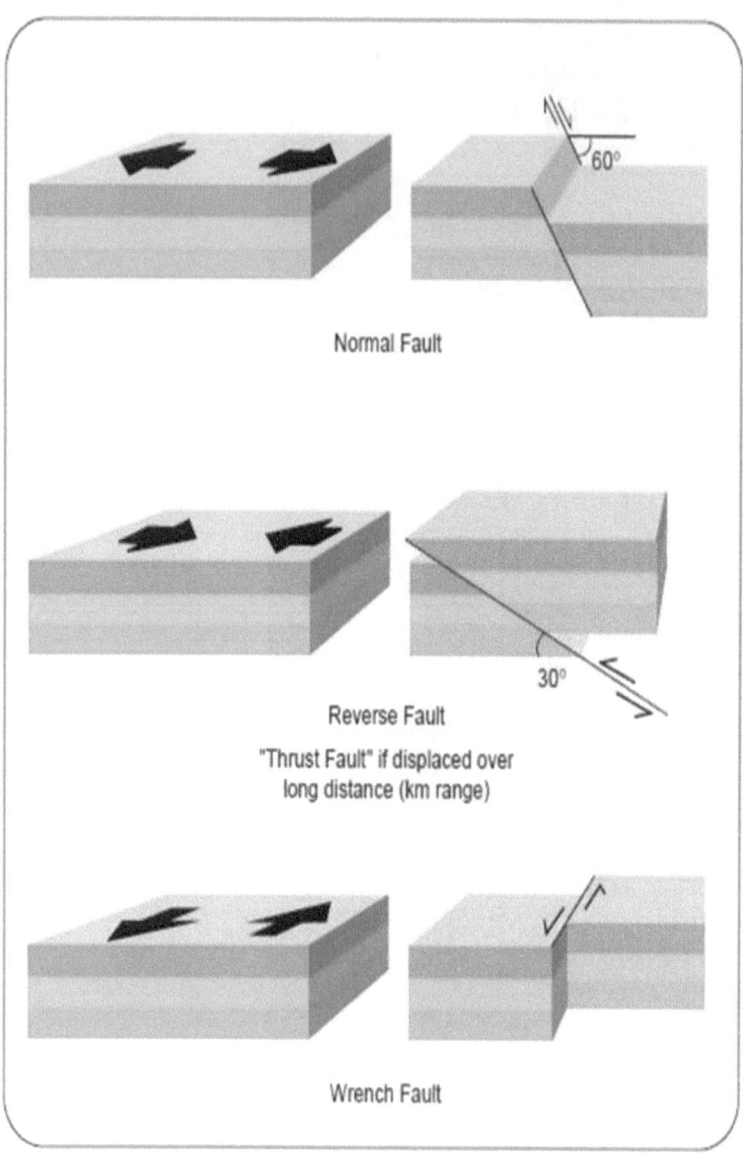

Normal Fault

Reverse Fault

"Thrust Fault" if displaced over long distance (km range)

Wrench Fault

Faults may extend over several hundreds of kilometers or may be restricted to the deformation of individual grains. They create vast potential traps for the accumulation of oil and gas. However, they often dissect reservoirs and seal fluid and pressures in numerous individual compartments. Each of these isolated blocks may require individual dedicated wells for production and injection. Reservoir compartmentalization through small-scale faulting can thus severely downgrade the profitability of a field under development. In the worst case, faulting is not detected until development is in an advanced stage. Early 3D seismic surveys will help to obtain a realistic assessment of fault density and possibly indicate the sealing potential of individual faults. However, small-scale faults with a displacement (throw) of less than some 5–10m are not detectable using seismic alone. Geostatistical techniques can then be used to predict their frequency and direction.

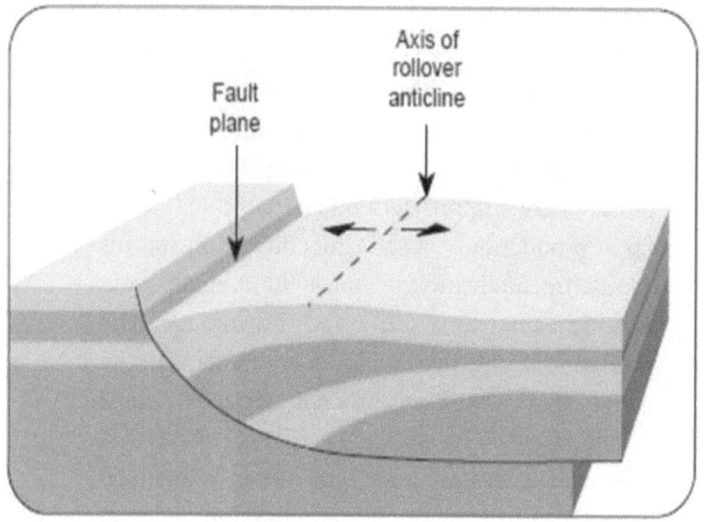

Four mechanisms have been suggested to explain how faults provide seals. The most frequent case is that of clay smear and juxtaposition:

_ Clay smear: soft clay, often of marine origin, is smeared into the fault plane during movement and provides an effective seal.

_ Juxtaposition: faulting has resulted in an impermeable rock 'juxtaposed' against a reservoir rock.

Other, less frequent fault seals are created by

_ Diagenetic healing: late precipitation of minerals on or near the fault plane has created a sealing surface.

_ Cataclasis: the fault movement has destroyed the rock matrix close to the fault plane. Individual quartz grains have been 'ground up' creating a seal comprising of 'rock flour'.

In many cases, faults will only restrict fluid flow, or they may be 'open', that is non-sealing. Despite considerable efforts to predict the probability of fault sealing potential, a wholly reliable method to do so has not yet emerged. Fault seal modelling is further complicated by the fact that some faults may leak fluids or pressures at a very small rate, thus effectively acting as seal on a production time scale of only a couple of years. As a result, the simulation of reservoir behavior in densely faulted fields is difficult and predictions should be regarded as crude approximations only.

Fault seals are known to have been ruptured by excessive differential pressures created by production operations, for example if the hydrocarbons of one block are produced whilst the next block is kept at original pressure. Uncontrolled cross-flow and inter-reservoir communication may be the result.

Whereas faults displace formerly connected lithologic units, fractures do not show appreciable displacement. They also represent planes of brittle failure and affect hard

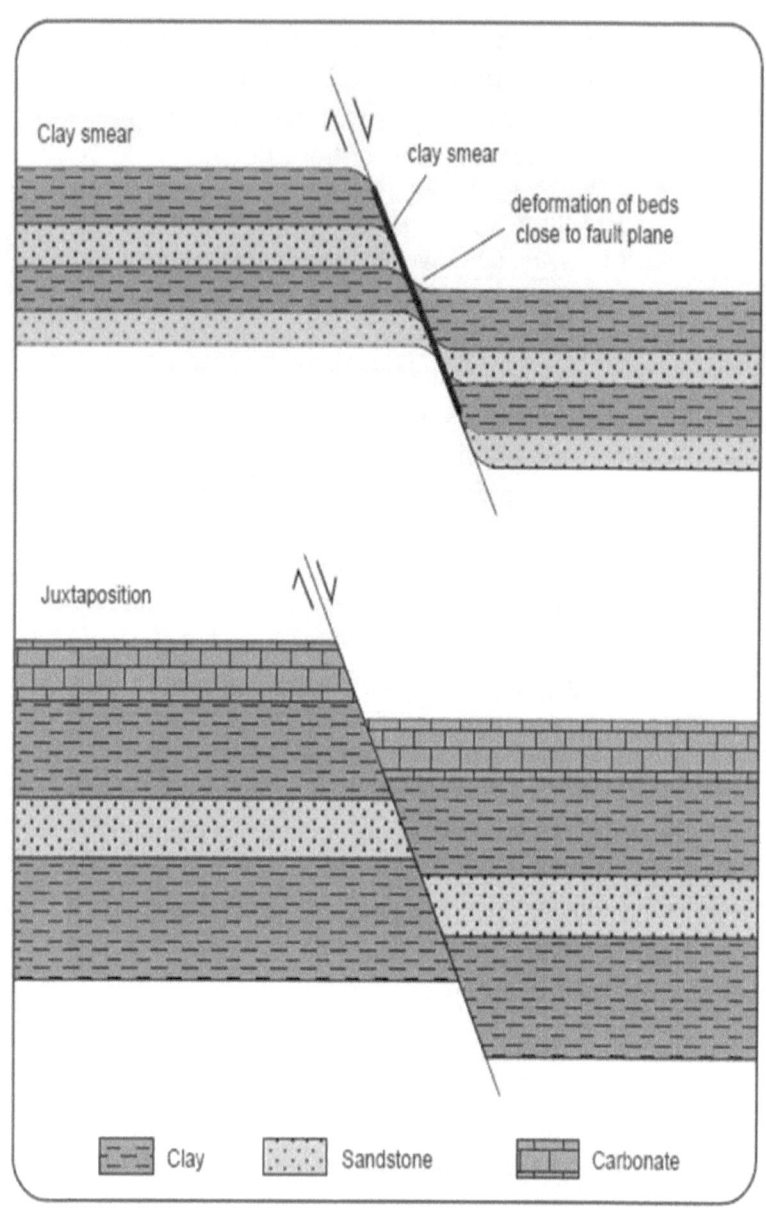

or competent lithologies rather than ductile or incompetent rocks such as claystone.

Frequently fractures are oriented normal to bedding planes. Carbonate rocks are more frequently fractured than sandstones. In many cases, open fractures in carbonate reservoirs provide high porosity/high permeability pathways for hydrocarbon production. The fractures will be continuously re-charged from the tight (less permeable) rock matrix. During field development, wells need to be planned to intersect as many natural fractures as possible, for example by drilling horizontal wells.

Folds are features related to compressional, ductile deformation. They form some of the largest reservoir structures known. A fold pair consists of anticline and syncline. [1]

---

[1] Frank Jahn, Mark Cook and Mark Graham: HYDROCARBON EXPLORATION AND PRODUCTION. 2ND EDITION. Elsevier B.V. 2008. P 105

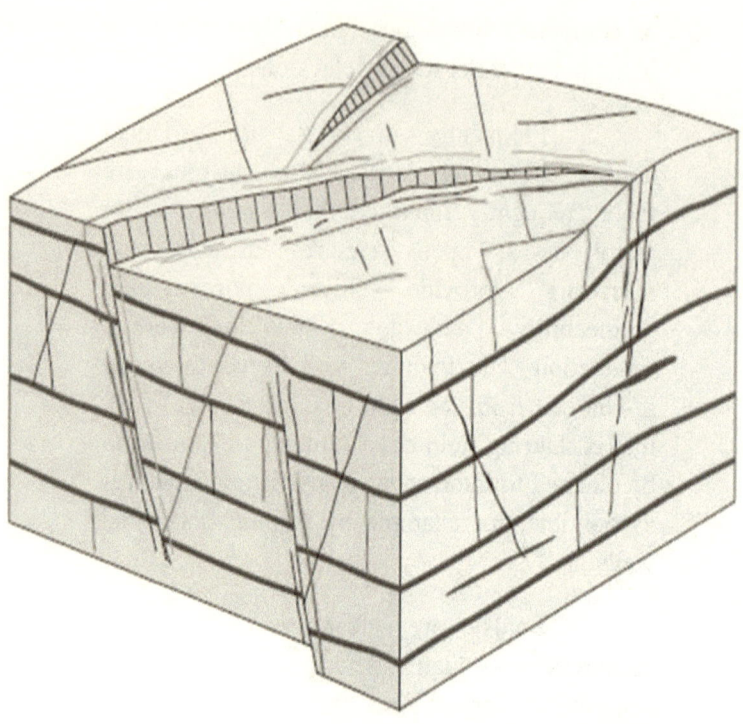

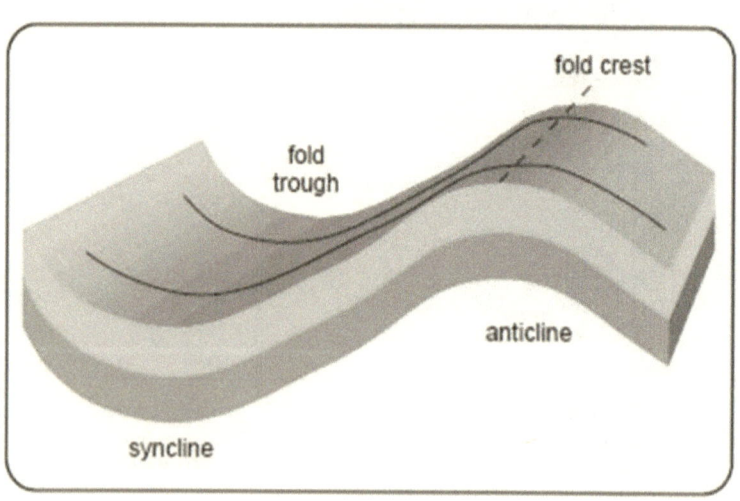

2. Reservoir Rocks

A rock capable of producing oil, gas, or water is called reservoir rock. A reservoir rock may be any rock with sufficient porosity and permeability to allow oil and gas to accumulate and be produced in commercial quantities. Petroleum generally occurs in sandstones, limestones, dolomites, conglomerates, and shales, but sometimes it is also found in igneous and metamorphic rocks. As a whole, sandstone and carbonate rocks are the most common reservoir rocks. However, reservoir rocks are quite variable in composition and physical properties. The physical properties of reservoir rocks are the vital information for producers to estimate the geological reserve and ultimate recovery of an oilfield and determine the most efficient method of petroleum production. [1]

Reservoir rocks may be investigated from two points of view, namely, microscopic and megascopic. If we study a core or a sample of a reservoir rock containing petroleum and place it under a magnifying glass (binocular or microscope), we can observe that the reservoir rock is made of a framework of minerals (rigid or friable) which fills but part of the void space. The void space in the rock is broadly known as

---

[1]Xuetao Hu • Shuyong Hu Fayang Jin • Su Huang: Physics of petroleum Reservoirs, Petroleum Industry Press, Beijing, China 2017. P 7

pore. Oil, gas, or/and water can enter and fill in the pores if they are interconnected. In general, interconnected pores are interlaced within the mineral framework. The size, quantity, and shape of the interconnected pores in a reservoir rock determine the ability of the rock storing and transmitting fluids. Therefore, the physical properties of reservoir rocks are in essence dependent on the mineral framework of the rock, namely on the mineral composition and the texture of the rock. [1]

Reservoir rocks are either of clastic or carbonate composition. The former is composed of silicates, usually sandstone, the latter of biogenetically derived detritus, such as coral or shell fragments. There are some important differences between the two rock types which affect the quality of the reservoir and its interaction with fluids which flow through them.

The main component of sandstone reservoirs (siliciclastic reservoirs) is quartz (SiO2). Chemically it is a fairly stable mineral which is not easily altered by changes in pressure, temperature or acidity of pore fluids. Sandstone reservoirs form after the sand grains have been transported over large distances and

---

[1]Xuetao Hu • Shuyong Hu Fayang Jin • Su Huang: Physics of petroleum Reservoirs, Petroleum Industry Press, Beijing, China 2017. P 7

have deposited in particular environments of deposition.

Carbonate reservoir rock is usually found at the place of formation (in situ). Carbonate rocks are susceptible to alteration by the processes of diagenesis.

The pores between the rock components, for example the sand grains in a sandstone reservoir, will initially be filled with the pore water. The migrating hydrocarbons will displace the water and thus gradually fill the reservoir. For a reservoir to be effective, the pores need to be in communication to allow migration, and also need to allow flow towards the borehole once a well is drilled into the structure. The pore space is referred to as porosity in oil field terms. Permeability measures the ability of a rock to allow fluid flow through its pore system. A reservoir rock which has some porosity but too low a permeability to allow fluid flow is termed 'tight'. [1]

Carbonate rocks are not normally transported over long distances, and we find carbonate reservoir rocks mostly at the location of origin, 'in situ'. They are usually the product of marine organisms. However, carbonates are

---

[1]Frank Jahn, Mark Cook and Mark Graham: HYDROCARBON EXPLORATION AND PRODUCTION. 2ND EDITION. Elsevier B.V. 2008. P 22: 23

often severely affected by diagenetic processes. [1]

2.1. Porosity of Reservoir Rocks

Choquette and Pray (1970) followed by Lucia (1995) established the main foundations of what is called today "Porogenesis", invoking the evolution of porosity during carbonate diagenesis.

The basic types of porosity in carbonate rocks were first grouped as fabric and not fabric selective. In the first category, primary porosity types include inter and intra-particle, fenestral, shelter and growth framework. Mouldic and intercrystalline porosity types are considered secondary (post-deposition) fabric-selective. Not fabric selective porosity types are all secondary and they include fractures, channels, vugs (and caverns). In addition, a genetic approach to the porosity development and evolution was achieved by providing clues regarding the major diagenetic process (cementation/filling versus dissolution) and its magnitude/extent. Lucia (1995) and later on Lønøy (2006) go even further and try to associate grain types (and size) to porosity types.

Using porosity/permeability relationships, they aimed to better understand

([1])Frank Jahn, Mark Cook and Mark Graham: HYDROCARBON EXPLORATION AND PRODUCTION. 2ND EDITION. Elsevier B.V. 2008. P 98

the permeability of carbonate rocks (attempts towards better rock-typing).

Decades ago, porosity was chiefly investigated by petrographers through microscopic examinations of thin-sections representing only 2D views of the three-dimensional pore space.

Petrophysicists measure independently the flow properties (e.g. MICP, Air-Permeability) of the same bulk rocks, hence taking into account the three-dimensional aspect of the macro-porosity.

Besides, wireline logs, petro-acoustic and seismic data are routinely used for modern reservoir characterization and rock-typing. This mismatch in analytical measurements (2D vs. 3D) brought a major challenge for precise quantitative description of flow properties (porosity and permeability) in carbonate rocks. It often represented a difficulty in integrated studies and communication between the petrographer, the petrophysicist and the reservoir engineer.

Today, with advances in X-ray computed tomography and new generations of scanning electron microscopes, the bridge between petrophysics and petrography has been provided.

The pore space can be investigated with 3D scanning and micro-scanning, and eventually linked to the 3D flow properties of sedimentary rocks.

Such approach is at the micro-scale and needs to be brought up to the scale of reservoirs. To do so, one major step remains and that is to constrain correctly the challenging representative elementary volumes (REV). Pore Network Modelling

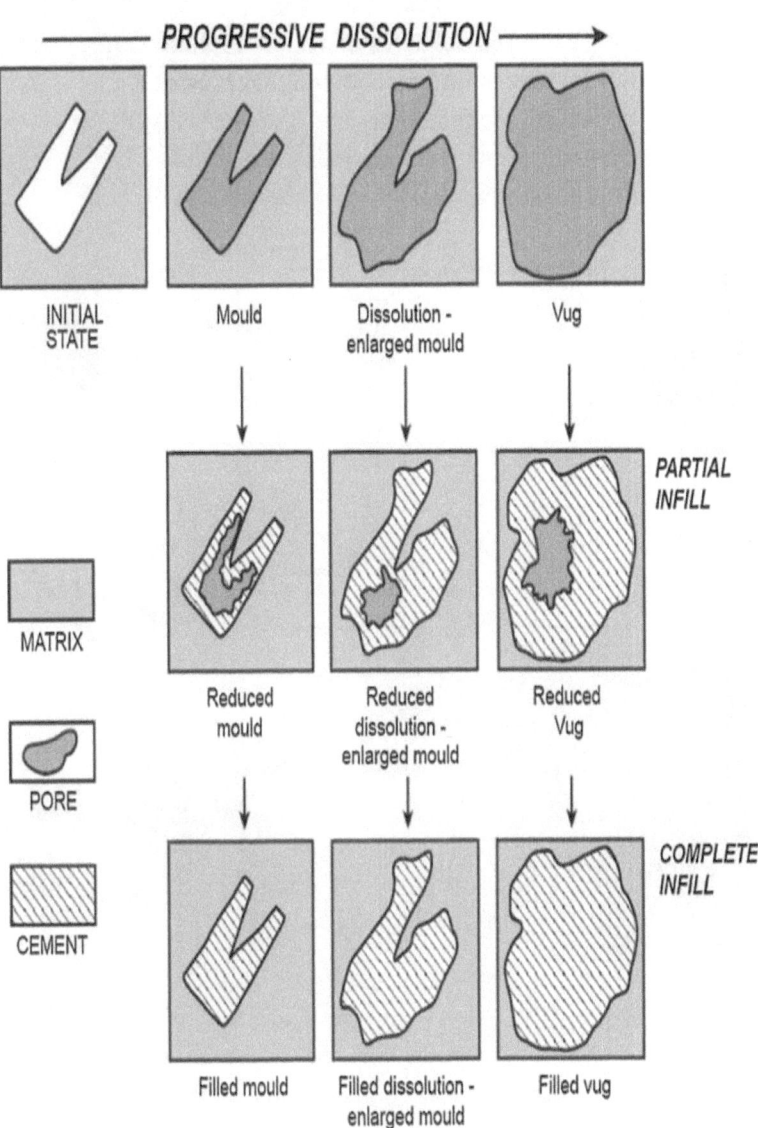

(PNM) can also be used to analyze the pore structure evolution in carbonate rocks. More recently reactive-PNM and micro-CT techniques have been used to investigate the evolution of flow properties influenced by diagenesis, e.g. dissolution/precipitation. Alternatively, numerical flow simulations can also be undertaken through 3D pore-space models. [1]

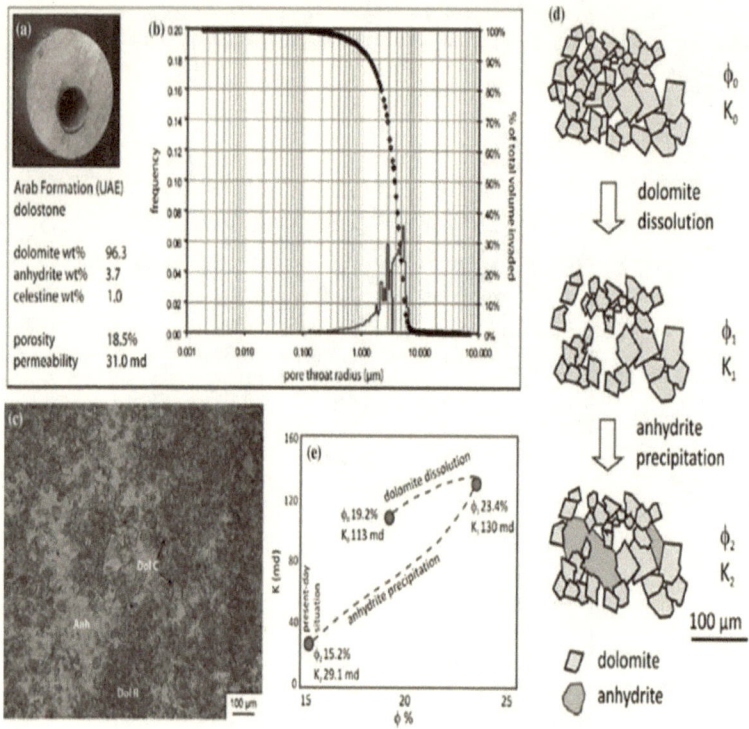

The first element of an oil/gas reservoir is the reservoir rock. The essential feature of a reservoir rock is porosity: the rock must contain pores or voids, which should be of

[1] Fadi Henri Nader: Multi-scale Quantitative Diagenesis and Impacts on Heterogeneity of Carbonate Reservoir Rocks. Springer International Publishing AG 2017. P 4: 7

such size and character as to permit the storage of oil and gas in reservoirs that are large enough to justify exploitation. Porosity, however, is not enough; the pores must be interconnected to permit the passage of oil and gas through the rock. In other words, the rock must be permeable (it is said to have permeability); otherwise there would be little if any accumulation into reservoirs, nor could any petroleum that accumulated be produced by drilling wells, as the accumulation of petroleum would not move into the wells fast enough. A pumice rock, for example, would not make a good reservoir even though the greater part of it might consist of pore space, for the pores are not interconnected and the porosity is not effective. The conventional shale generally cannot become a reservoir rock, for the pores are so tiny that the capillary attraction of the fluids for the mineral grains effectively holds the fluids in the rock. Trying to get petroleum out of a shale would be like trying to remove ink from a blotter. Therefore, the porosity and the pore structure of reservoir rocks are the key factors to affect the quality of reservoirs and control the off-take potentials of oil or gas wells. [1]

  The development of oil and gas reservoirs shows that the void space holding oil

---

[1]Xuetao Hu • Shuyong Hu Fayang Jin • Su Huang: Physics of petroleum Reservoirs, Petroleum Industry Press, Beijing, China 2017. P 25

or gas is only small part of whole rock volume. Oil or gas is not in the underground lakes or streams of oil which once was a popular idea. Porosity is a measure of the void space of reservoir rocks, and thus represents the storage capacity of the reservoirs. Porosity is the best-known physical characteristic of petroleum reservoirs.

Porosity is very important rock property because it can be used to measure the potential volume of hydrocarbons in reservoir rocks. All recovery computations must be based on the knowledge of this parameter. It is one of the most important reservoir parameters in the study of petroleum reservoir engineering. [1]

Reservoir porosity can be measured directly from core samples or indirectly using logs. However, as core coverage is rarely complete, logging is the most common method employed, and the results are compared against measured core porosities where core material is available.

The formation density log is the main tool for measuring porosity. It measures the bulk density of a small volume of formation in front of the logging tool, which is a mixture of minerals and fluids. Provided the rock matrix

---

[1] Xuetao Hu • Shuyong Hu Fayang Jin • Su Huang: Physics of petroleum Reservoirs, Petroleum Industry Press, Beijing, China 2017. P 39

and fluid densities are known, the relative proportion of rock and fluid (and hence porosity) can be determined.

The density tool is constructed so that medium-energy GRs are directed from a radioactive source into the formation. These GRs interact with the formation by a process known as Compton scattering, in which GRs lose energy each time they collide with an electron. The number of GRs reaching detectors in the tool is inversely proportional to the number of electrons (or the electron density) in the formation, which is related to the formation bulk density. A low GR count implies a high electron (and bulk) density and therefore a low porosity.

The bulk density measured by the logging tool is the weighted average of the rock matrix and fluid densities, so that

$$\rho_b = \rho_f \phi + \rho_{ma}(1 - \phi)$$

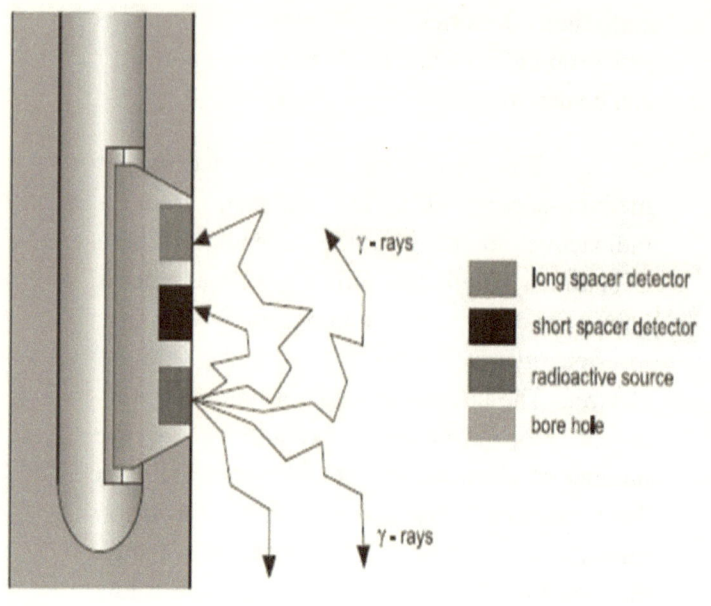

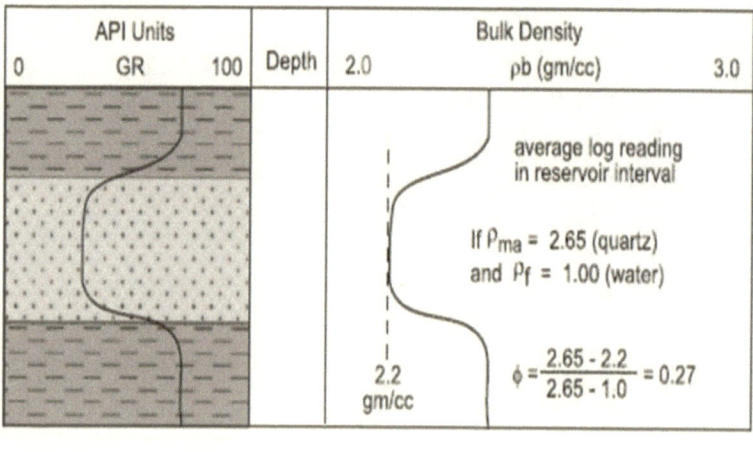

The formation bulk density (p_b) can be read directly from the density log and the matrix density (p_{ma}) and fluid density (p_f) found in tables, assuming we have already identified lithology and fluid content from other measurements.

The equation can be rearranged for porosity (f) as follows:

$$\phi = \frac{\rho_{ma} - \rho_b}{\rho_{ma} - \rho_f}$$

Other logging tools which can be used to determine porosity include the neutron, sonic and NMR tools. The neutron tool has a design similar to the density tool except that it employs neutrons instead of GRs. The neutrons are slowed down as they travel through the formation and some are captured. Of the common reservoir elements, hydrogen has the greatest stopping power. A low count rate at the detector indicates large number of hydrogen atoms in the formation and, as hydrogen is present in water and oil in similar amounts, implies high porosity.

Because the neutron tool responds to hydrogen it can be used to differentiate between gas and liquids (oil or water) in the formation. A specific volume of gas will contain a lot fewer hydrogen atoms than the same volume of oil or water (at the same pressure), and therefore in a gas-bearing reservoir the neutron porosity (which assumes the tool is investigating fluid-filled formation) will register an artificially low porosity. A large apparent decrease in porosity in the upper section of a homogenous reservoir interval is often indicative of entering gas-bearing formation.

The sonic tool measures the time taken for a sound wave to pass through the formation. Sound waves travel in high-density (i.e. low porosity) formation faster than in low-density (high porosity) formation. The porosity can be determined by measuring the transit time for the sound wave to travel between a transmitter and receiver, provided the rock matrix and fluid are known.

The NMR tool magnetically aligns hydrogen protons and then measures the time taken for this alignment to decay. In a reservoir the hydrogen atoms occur chiefly in the fluid as either water or hydrocarbon within the pore space. The speed of decay is proportional to the size of the pore. Hence the NMR tool can not only determine porosity but also indicate the pore size distribution. [1]

2.2. Petrography

Petrographic analyses remain the basics of any diagenetic study. Carbonate rocks

[1] Frank Jahn, Mark Cook and Mark Graham: HYDROCARBON EXPLORATION AND PRODUCTION. 2ND EDITION. Elsevier B.V. 2008. P 161: 163

are investigated routinely with microscopic techniques to

describe their textures, fabrics, and porosity. The various diagenetic features (replacive minerals, cements, dissolution, pressure-solution, etc.), are detailed and placed in chronological order based on cross-cutting relationships. Subsequently, a

Sections locations	Samples (thin sections)	AAS	AES	O/C isotopes (sequential)	Sr isotopes	XRD	Wafers	Crush-leach
Jeita-Metn	226 (160)	140	14	125 (21)	19	33	8	12
N. Ibrahim	191 (106)	48		83 (2)	2	25	4	5
Qadisha	83 (32)	42		56		14		
Total	500 (241)	230	14	264 (23)	21	72	12	17

Para genesis is proposed and will be further refined with geochemical and mineralogical investigations as well as fluid inclusions analysis.

Samples are systematically subjected to preliminary preparation and 'pre-microscopic' observation (of cut-faces) before thin section preparation and subsequent conventional microscopic examination (Nader 2003). In general, plugs are less often processed through this scheme, and frequently anticipated to thin section preparation.

2.2.1. Pre-microscopic Observations

'Pre-microscopic observations' encompass a series of steps necessary for providing larger scale petrological information of a sample.

Accordingly, sample preparation first consists of sawing the pieces or plugs in order to produce flat cut-faces or 'slabs', which are then processed for polishing, etching, staining (and peeling, see Nader 2003), all combined with low magnification binocular macroscopic investigation. Staining carbonate rock slabs is usually done by applying a solution of potassium ferricyanide blue and alizarin red S (Dickson 1966). This is done in order to distinguish (ferroan) calcite and (ferroan) dolomite. Other types of solution may be used to distinguish other minerals.

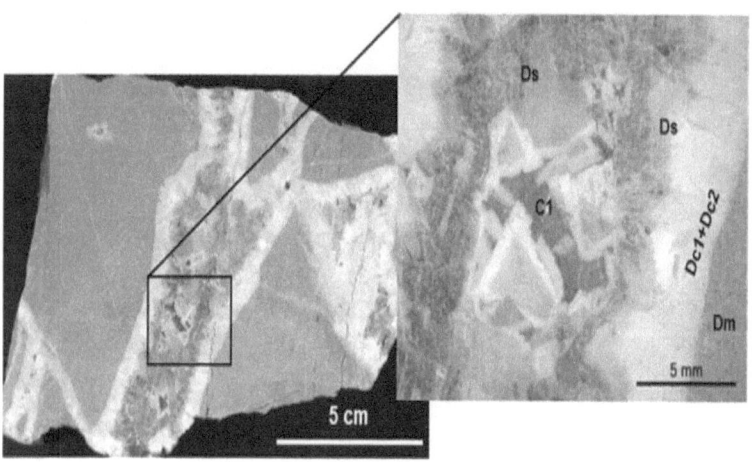

Recently the computerized tomography CT technique provides the possibility to scan bulk rocks (or well cores) in 3D in order to select the optimal sampling locations, before destroying the bulk sample. Then, smaller plugs can be drilled out of the bulk rocks and scanned with higher resolution. This technique should also be coupled with classical microscopic investigations.

2.2.2. Microscopic Observations

Cathodoluminescence is simply the luminescence emitted by minerals when they are excited with radiation caused by an electron beam. Microscopic viewing under fluorescent light can be used to investigate organic matter, to emphasis the porosity of carbonate rocks (impregnated with fluorescent dye), and to identify HC-rich fluid inclusions. Both fluorescence and cathodoluminescence (CL) microscopy should only be performed after the completion of conventional microscopic examination. Usually, for each CL and fluorescence photomicrograph a transmitted-light double is also taken. These techniques proved to be very useful for pre-set targets (e.g. determination of specific cement types, emphasis porosity, comparison between similar diagenetic phases present in different samples, assessing the homogeneity of the sample for precise isotopic and/or chemical analyses).

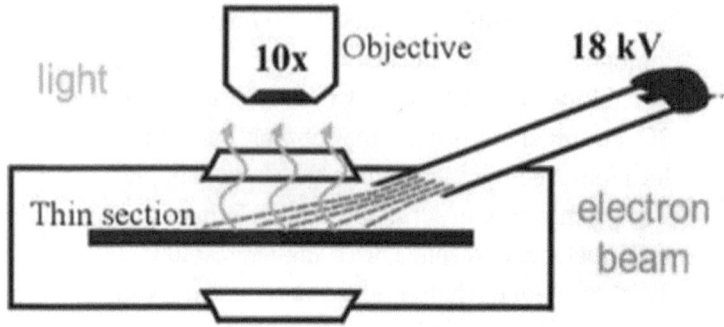

Scanning electron microscopy (SEM) is a technique that allows the petrographic examination under three-dimensional viewing and higher magnifications (10–100,000 times). The relatively old JEOL-JSM 6400 Scanning Electron Microscope unit is an example of SEM devices with operating conditions of 15–40 kV accelerating voltage, 2.10^{-7} to 10^{-9} A probe current, and working distance of 8–39 mm. The newer, EVO MA10 Zeiss SMT equipment has a computer-motorized five axis stage, enabling rapid sample observation. It operates with a tungsten filament at 15 kV and 100 mA, and a probe current of 150–700 pA (for SE imaging and EDS analysis, respectively). Combined with an Energy Dispersive X-ray Spectrometer (EDS), relative determination of compositional elements, based on the X-ray energy, may be performed.

The SEM works by producing a high energetic electron beam in vacuum (inside an electron gun; LaB6 or tungsten filament) that is accelerated towards the specimen surface. The electron bombardment of the specimen surface results in two types of electrons—low energy secondary electrons (SE) and high energy backscatter electrons (BE). The former electrons are captured in a photomultiplier tube and transformed into an image on the screen, while the latter backscatter electrons (BE) are used to detect compositional variations (given that the intensity of the BE is composition dependent, i.e. related to the mean atomic number of the target).

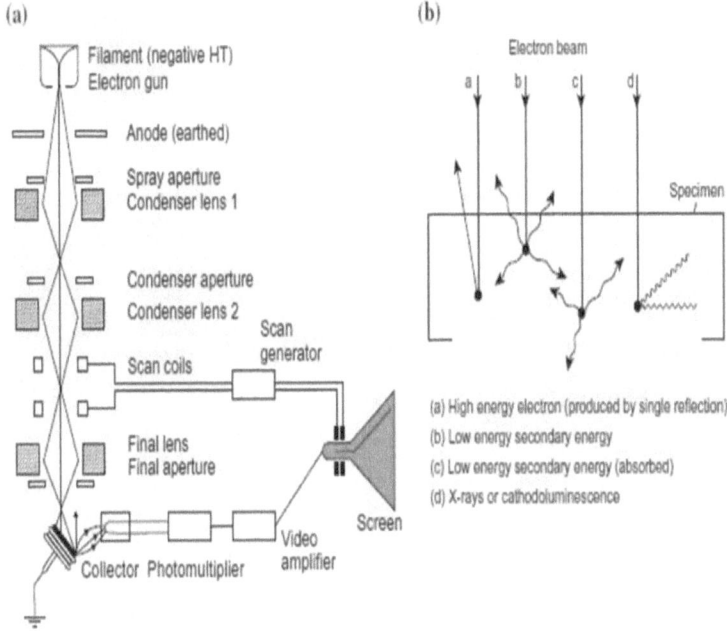

High resolution 2D compositional analyses are performed with new SEM-EDS (and/or microprobes; EPMA) equipment (e.g. Zeiss EVO SEM, Oxford ESS), by applying punctual analysis for chemical composition and mineral mapping on thin-sections. The time counting of 1000 microseconds can be set for spectral imaging, and the acquisition time for 86 _ 128 pixels in the order of 1 h 30 min. Accordingly, mineral assemblages can be mapped, and the porosity change associated to mineralogical transformations through diagenesis can be determined.

X-ray intensity maps of all elements are transformed to oxide wt.% by means of software packages (e.g. AZtecEnergy, produced by Oxford Instruments) constrained by EDS standardization.

Statistical cluster analysis is commonly used to identify the different phases occurring in the samples (see below). Data output (from SEM-EDS analyses) can be further analyzed with MatlabTM software based on De Andrade et al. (2006). [1]

---

[1]Fadi Henri Nader: Multi-scale Quantitative Diagenesis and Impacts on Heterogeneity of Carbonate Reservoir Rocks. Springer International Publishing AG 2017. P 17: 20

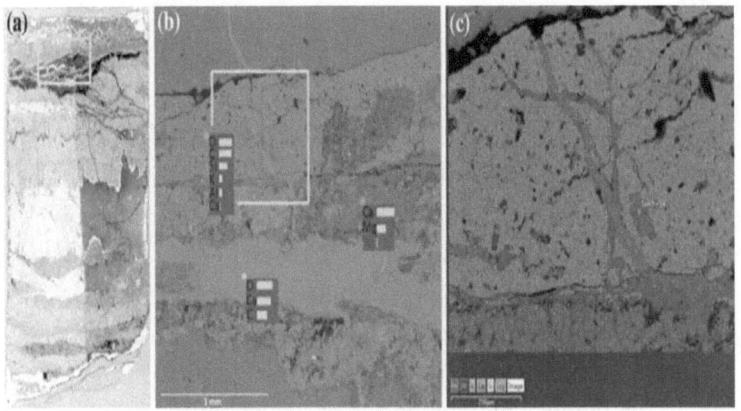

2.3. Permeability of Reservoir Rocks

In addition to porosity, permeability is also a rock property depending on the pore space of rocks. However, permeability is a measure of the ability of a rock to transmit fluids through the pore network in the rock whereas porosity just characterizes the capacity of the rock holding fluids. In petroleum reservoirs, rock permeability is one of the most valuable characteristics that the reservoir engineer seeks to determine. The oil in a reservoir rock can be extracted through bore holes only if the rock is permeable. A solid of no porosity would be impermeable to a fluid, and it is also possible for a rock of high porosity to be impermeable, namely zero permeability. Such a rock, though saturated with oil will give no production when the reservoir is drilled. [1]

---

[1] Xuetao Hu • Shuyong Hu Fayang Jin • Su Huang: Physics of petroleum Reservoirs, Petroleum Industry Press,

Permeability, as the name implies (ability to permeate), is a measure of how easily a fluid can flow through a rock. It is a critical property in defining the flow capacity of a rock. The study of permeability is perhaps the most important single study in the science of petroleum production. Without a sound knowledge of the permeability of a reservoir, it is impossible to estimate the probable rate of production of oil or the best methods of economic production. Consequentially, rock permeability is an indispensable basic parameter of reservoirs for the oil production and the dynamic investigation of petroleum reservoir engineering. [1]

2.4. Compressibility of Reservoir Rocks

Rocks when buried at reservoir depths are subject to both internal and external stresses. The internal stress results from the pressure of fluids in rock pores. The external stresses are exerted by the weight of the overburden (overlying formations) and any accompanying tectonic stresses. Overburden pressures vary from area to area depending on factors such as depth, nature of the structure, consolidation of the formation, and possibly the geologic age and history of the rocks. Depth of the formation is

---

Beijing, China 2017. P 84
[1]Xuetao Hu • Shuyong Hu Fayang Jin • Su Huang: Physics of petroleum Reservoirs, Petroleum Industry Press, Beijing, China 2017. P 84

the most important consideration, and a typical value of overburden pressure is approximately 0.023 MPa per meter of depth. [1]

The weight of the overburden simply applies a compressive force to the reservoir. The pressure in the rock pore spaces does not normally approach the overburden pressure. A typical pore pressure, commonly referred to as the reservoir pressure, is approximately 0.01 MPa per meter of depth, assuming that the reservoir is sufficiently consolidated so the overburden pressure is not transmitted to the fluids in the pore spaces.

Before production, internal pressure (pore pressure) and external pressure (overburden pressure, confining pressure) in reservoirs maintain balance each other. Once the reservoir is disturbed by drilling and consequently production, the pressure balance is broken.

The pressure difference between overburden and internal pore pressure is referred to as the effective overburden pressure. During pressure depletion (oil reservoir production), the initial pore pressure decreases and the effective overburden pressure increases since the overburden load remains constant. This increase

---

[1]Xuetao Hu • Shuyong Hu Fayang Jin • Su Huang: Physics of petroleum Reservoirs, Petroleum Industry Press, Beijing, China 2017. P 63

in pressure difference causes the following effects: [1]

(a) The bulk volume of the reservoir rock is reduced;

(b) Sand grains constituting the rock expand;

(c) Fluids within the pore spaces expand.

The first two volume changes tend to reduce the pore space of the rock.

Obviously, both the decrease in pore volume and the expansion of fluids will continuously drive fluids flowing out from pores. Moreover, the output of fluids from the reservoirs will lead to the farther decline in pore pressure and the release of the elastic energies of rock and fluids. The elastic energy of a rock is actually an exhibition of rock compressibility. The elastic energies from the rock and fluids are thus the major drive energies of oil production in an undersaturated oil reservoir, especially in the initial stage of reservoir production. [2]

---

[1] Xuetao Hu • Shuyong Hu Fayang Jin • Su Huang: Physics of petroleum Reservoirs, Petroleum Industry Press, Beijing, China 2017. P 63: 64

[2] Xuetao Hu • Shuyong Hu Fayang Jin • Su Huang: Physics of petroleum Reservoirs, Petroleum Industry Press, Beijing, China 2017. P 64

2.5. Sensitivity of Reservoir Rocks

In reservoir rocks, there are always some minerals which are sensitive to some factors (such as invading fluids, flow rate, and so on) and thus cause a decrease in reservoir permeability in the process of oil/gas production. This phenomenon is known as formation/reservoir damage or reservoir sensitivity. Formation damage is an undesirable operational and economic problem that can occur during the various phases of an oil/gas reservoir life time, including well drilling, hydraulic fracturing, oil/gas production, workover operations, etc. Formation damage may be caused by various processes, including chemical, physical, biological, and thermal interactions of formation and fluids, and deformation of formation under stress and fluid shear. In order to avoid, control, and remedy formation damage, the sensitivity of reservoir rocks needs to well understood. And various properly experimental techniques are necessary to evaluate the sensitivity of petroleum reservoirs.

In sandstones, rock sensitivity is mainly caused by cementing agents in rocks. The sensitivity of reservoir rocks is thus dependent on the components, content, and distribution of cementing agents in sandstones. [1]

2.6. Assessment Methods of Reservoir Sensitivity

In general, petroleum reservoir may have several kinds of sensitivity, typically including water sensitivity, salinity sensitivity, acid sensitivity, alkali sensitivity, and flow velocity sensitivity. The evaluation on reservoir sensitivity chiefly focuses on the effects of physical-chemical reactions between invading fluids and the rock on the permeability of the rock. Systematical evaluation for reservoir sensitivity includes a series of experimental analysis, e.g., petrology analysis, conventional core analysis, special core analysis, core flow testing, and so on. The measurement of reservoir sensitivity is primarily based on the core flow testing. [1]

2.7. Types of Reservoir Space

In petroleum reservoirs, reservoir space means the void system which can hold gas or oil. Reservoir space may be composed of one of the three void types: pore, fracture, dissolved cavern, or free combination of the three void types. Reservoir space is thus complicated. Different combinations of void types form

---

[1]Xuetao Hu • Shuyong Hu Fayang Jin • Su Huang: Physics of petroleum Reservoirs, Petroleum Industry Press, Beijing, China 2017. P 126

[1]Xuetao Hu • Shuyong Hu Fayang Jin • Su Huang: Physics of petroleum Reservoirs, Petroleum Industry Press, Beijing, China 2017. P 148

different types of reservoir space, in which fluids have different flow patterns. Both the types of reservoir space and flow patterns of fluids are very concerned by reservoir engineers, they are the important foundation of reservoir engineering calculation and have a great effect on the oil recovery. [1]

Based on the combination type of voids, reservoir space of petroleum reservoirs can be classified as: single-porosity medium, dual-porosity medium, and triple-porosity medium.

Single-porosity medium means that the reservoir space of petroleum reservoirs consists of one type of voids. It may be single-pore, single-fracture, or single-dissolved cavern system. In this kind of reservoir, fluids are held and flow in the same void space.

The reservoir of dual-porosity medium has two types of voids. It may be pore-fracture system, dissolved cavern-pore system, or fracture-dissolved cavern system. For example, if a rock contains both fracture network and intergranular pores (e.g., a sandstone), the rock is called dual-porosity medium.

---

[1] Xuetao Hu • Shuyong Hu Fayang Jin • Su Huang: Physics of petroleum Reservoirs, Petroleum Industry Press, Beijing, China 2017. P 33

In a dual-porosity reservoir, such as a pore-fracture reservoir, the pores are customarily the space holding oil or gas, whereas the fracture network mainly acts as the flow passage of oil or gas. The flow through the fractures is accompanied by the exchange of fluid from and to the surrounding porous rock matrix. Exchange between the fracture network and the porous block (matrix) is normally represented by a term that describes the rate of mass transfer. The physical parameters of both the fracture and block are needed to be defined at each mathematical point in the flow domain. As a result, dual porosity and dual permeability are necessary to characterize the properties of this kind of reservoir. At present, this kind of reservoir is mainly found in carbonate rock, especially in limestone or dolomite. Such reservoirs exist extensively in carbonate rocks in Sichuan gas field of China.

Triple-porosity medium is the most complicated petroleum reservoir. It consists of three types of voids: intergranular pore, fracture and dissolved cavern/solution cavity. In this reservoir, the flow mechanism of fluids in each type of voids is different. Triple-porosity mediums have been found in Tahe oil field in Western China. [1]

---

[1]Xuetao Hu • Shuyong Hu Fayang Jin • Su Huang: Physics of petroleum Reservoirs, Petroleum Industry Press, Beijing, China 2017. P 33

2.8. Buried Depth and Compaction

With the increase in depth of reservoir rocks, geostatic pressure and formation temperature gradually increase, the grain arrangement thus becomes more compact. This change means the inelastic and irreversible locomotion occurring on the grain arrangement, the porosity of the rock is then sharp declined. [1]

As overburden pressure is increasing, grains in rocks become increasingly compact. The partial pressolution occurs at the places where grains contact each other. However, dissolved minerals, such as quartz, may also form new crystals in pore, which leads to a further decrease in porosity. In severe cases, it can cause pores to disappear and a rock to lose its permeability.

The porosity of carbonate rocks also decreases remarkably with the decrease in depth. Research shows that carbonate sediments deposit in a quite confined environment and have close relationship with biological action. After diagenesis, carbonate rocks are susceptible to various physicochemical changes in different environments, such as dissolution under groundwater, recrystallization under appropriate temperature and pressure, etc. As a result,

---

[1]Xuetao Hu • Shuyong Hu Fayang Jin • Su Huang: Physics of petroleum Reservoirs, Petroleum Industry Press, Beijing, China 2017. P 49

multifarious pore patterns may be formed in carbonate rocks; and primary porosity are easy to change because of the effects of environments. [1]

2.9. Fluid Saturation of Reservoir Rocks

the fluid phase can contain different constituents: typically, water, oil, and gas. However, the elastic properties of water, oil, and gas depend on a number of factors: temperature, pressure, water salinity, gas-oil ratio,

---

[1]Xuetao Hu • Shuyong Hu Fayang Jin • Su Huang: Physics of petroleum Reservoirs, Petroleum Industry Press, Beijing, China 2017. P 49

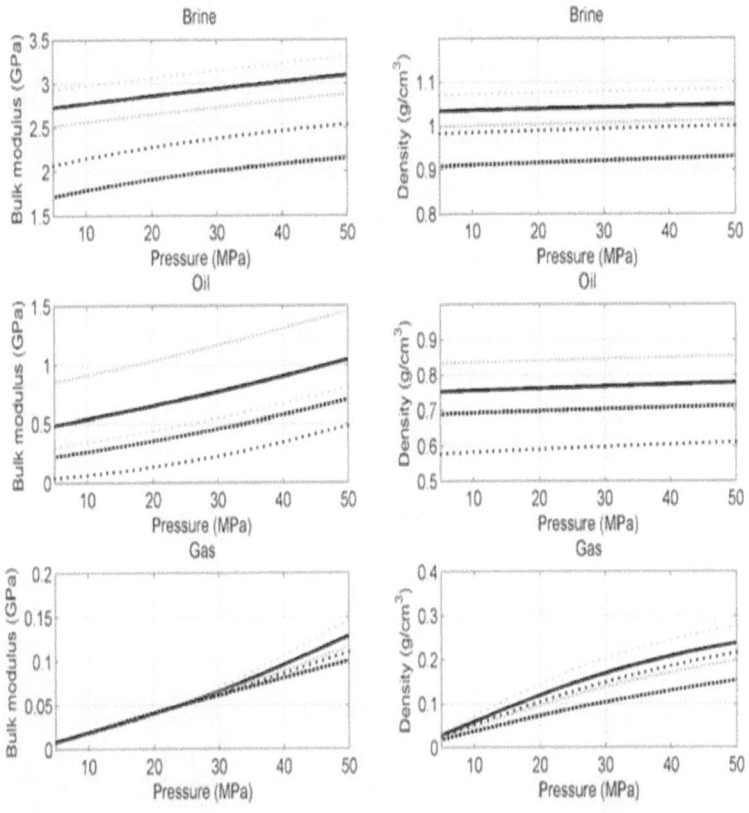

gas gravity, and oil gravity. Batzle and Wang derived a set of empirical models to link these variables to bulk moduli and density for different fluid types. For a complete mathematical formulation of these equations, we refer the reader to the original paper. In Fig., we show a sensitivity analysis to show the effects of the reservoir and fluid conditions on the bulk moduli and densities of the three main fluid types. [1]

Trapped fluids within crystals may well be petroleum. Petroleum fluid inclusions constitute excellent evidence associated to the oil/gas charge of reservoirs. Today, micro thermometry, confocal laser scanning microscopy and Raman micro spectroscopy are frequently used to investigate both aqueous/brine and petroleum inclusions and to associate them to diagenetic phases and petroleum systems. Combined to 1D burial modelling, timing of trapping such inclusions can also be defined.

In some mineral phases (e.g. fracture-filling cement), inclusions may contain liquid water plus vapor and liquid petroleum plus vapor, or even the three together. These fluid inclusions are highly valuable, as they may allow the estimation of trapping temperatures and pressures from homogenization temperatures by using the crossed isochores method (e.g. Emery and Robinson 1993). Assumption of PVT properties of the petroleum inclusions has to be done, usually on the basis that they correspond to the petroleum found (and produced) in the field. The liquid water nature might be also estimated by micro thermometry. Besides, both liquid petroleum and liquid water in a single inclusion are supposed to have been

---

([1])Congrui Jin • Gianluca Cusatis: New Frontiers in Oil and Gas Exploration. Springer International Publishing Switzerland 2016. P 145: 146

trapped together (i.e. at the same time). The intersection of the two sets of isochores represents the range of pressures and temperatures within which all inclusions should have been trapped. Note that usually the resulting values are exaggerated (i.e. higher than real values).

The scenario of petroleum and water trapped in co-precipitated minerals during the filling of a reservoir—with the assumption that the related fluid inclusions were unaltered after trapping— has also been simulated in the laboratory. Due to pressure or temperature stress, occurring after trapping, the fluid inclusions usually re-equilibrate by stretching (i.e. volumes of inclusions increase) and/or by leakage (i.e. loss of fluid). Such fluid inclusions record only the last maximum stress event with a new set of PVTx conditions.

Commonly, fluid inclusion analysis is combined with numerical burial models (1D). The pressure and temperature conditions at the trapping time can be further constrained (with evidence of larger basin-scale). The hydrostatic or lithostatic pressure regime during trapping can be as such estimated on the related PT diagram.

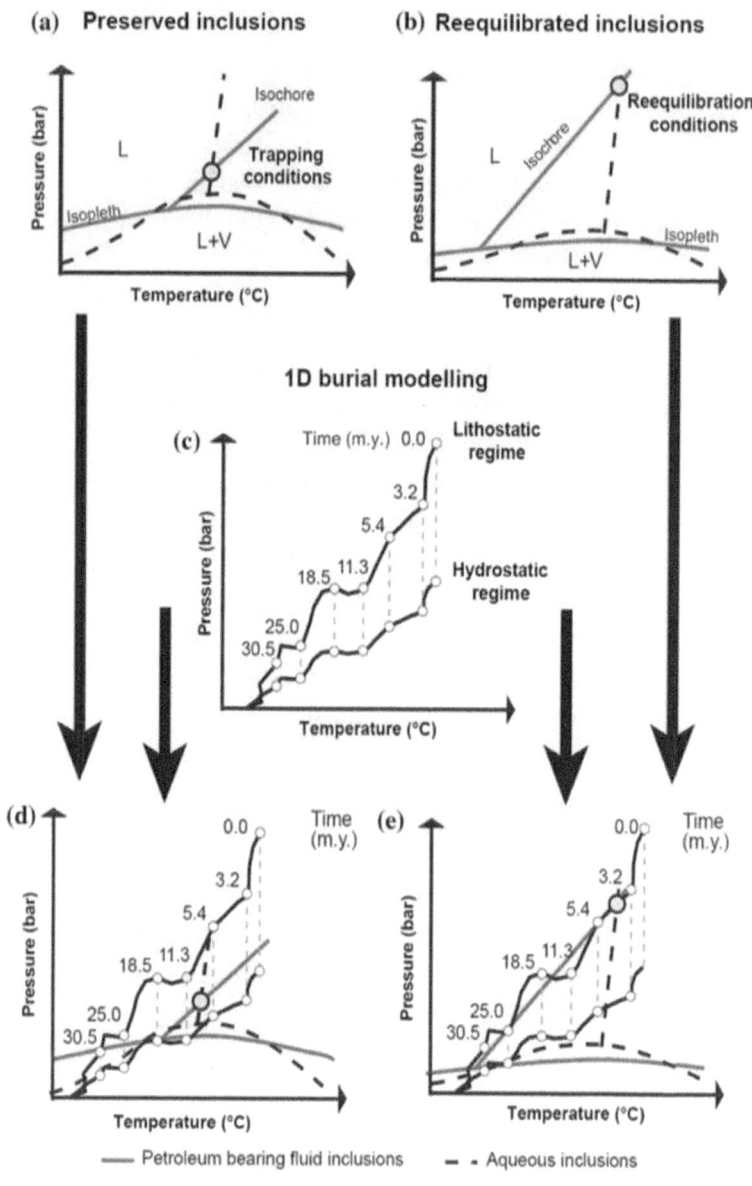

Here, isopleths and isochores of unaltered and re-equilibrated aqueous and petroleum fluid inclusions can be plot. The intersections of isochores correspond to the trapping PT conditions for the unaltered (preserved) inclusions and the later stress event for the requilibrated ones. Since, the evolution of the pressure regimes (hydrostatic and lithostatic) and temperature can be calculated by 1D burial modelling, one needs simply to combine both methods. Thereafter, the isochores intersection point of the unaltered inclusions, in the area between hydrostatic and lithostatic curves defines the pressure and temperature, as well as the time of trapping. The timing of the last maximum pressure and/or temperature stress is defined similarly for the re-equilibrated fluid inclusions.

Ong (2013) provided new insights on the diagenesis of the deeply buried siliciclastic reservoirs of oil fields in the Viking Graben (North Sea) by similar fluid inclusion analyses combined with burial modelling. PVTx of fluid inclusion trapping together with numerical basin modelling allowed indeed the reconstruction of fluid migration pathways associated with fluid overpressures in the investigated reservoir (Ong et al. 2014). Hence, the impact of basin-scale regional fluids on diagenesis and reservoir properties could be estimated.

Probably the most interesting advancement of the techniques related to fluid inclusion analysis concerns the experimental procedures. Synthetic analogues of aqueous fluid inclusions (e.g. FSCC, Fused Silica Capillary Capsule; Chou et al. 2008) have been used to mimic fluid inclusions. Thus, a mineral can be made to trap fluids at specific temperature and pressure conditions. Somehow, this approach may represent what happens at the scale of an oil/gas field and can also be used to constrain basin models.

Girard et al. (2014), presented at the "Journée Thématique ASF" conference on the 4th of July 2014 in Paris, a powerful new approach (the PIT-AIT) that consists of the synthesizing co-genetic petroleum and aqueous fluid inclusions and reconstructing their pressure and temperature paths. Henceforth, applications of this approach are to be applied to petroleum reservoirs and is capable to constrain the timing of the hydrocarbon charge, overpressure development as well as the exact P-T conditions of trapping. [1]

The saturation of reservoir fluids is another important physical property of reservoir rocks. The knowledge of fluid saturation is much

---

[1]Fadi Henri Nader: Multi-scale Quantitative Diagenesis and Impacts on Heterogeneity of Carbonate Reservoir Rocks. Springer International Publishing AG 2017. P 55: 57

necessary in every phase of reservoir production. For example, it is used for the estimation of initial oil or gas in place, i.e., geological reserves, at discovery stage, and for the identification of reservoir zones where a large quantity of oil is left behind. It is also involved in the evaluation of the enhanced oil recovery process. [1]

The pores in petroleum reservoirs are always completely saturated with fluids. In general, most rocks are completely saturated with groundwater. Under the right conditions, some of the pores in rocks may be occupied by other liquids, such oil or/and gas. In reservoir pores, actually, there is never an occasion or location where nothing exists (i.e., truly "void space"). In petroleum reservoirs, the pores may be completely filled with the following fluids: (1) oil and its associated impurities in the liquid phase; (2) natural gas and its associated impurities in the vapor phase; (3) water—either connate water or water that flowed or was injected into the reservoir. Because of the difference between the specific gravities of fluids, reservoirs exhibit dominance of a particular fluid saturation at different depths. For example, an oil zone having high oil saturation

---

[1]Xuetao Hu • Shuyong Hu Fayang Jin • Su Huang: Physics of petroleum Reservoirs, Petroleum Industry Press, Beijing, China 2017. P 68

can be overlain by a gas cap and underlain by formation water.

During the development of oil reservoirs, it is basically concerned that the volumes occupied by oil, gas, and water severally as these volumes represent the amount of oil, gas, and water in reservoirs. The quantity of a liquid in rock pores can be described by the term, saturation. The relative amounts of oil, gas, or water when more than one phase is present in the rock can then be characterized by individual phase saturation. [1]

After production, fluid saturations in a reservoir will alter significantly with time. This phenomenon can be observed due to the appearance of a new phase (such as free gas in oil reservoir or condensate liquid in gas reservoir). It can also be found following the injection of a driving fluid (such as water or gas) to enhance oil recovery. [2]

The common belief is that a reservoir initially saturated by water; then the oil comes from migration, and the water is expelled from the reservoir and replaced by oil that fills the pores in the reservoir rock. Practically, the water

---

[1] Xuetao Hu • Shuyong Hu Fayang Jin • Su Huang: Physics of petroleum Reservoirs, Petroleum Industry Press, Beijing, China 2017. P 68

[2] Xuetao Hu • Shuyong Hu Fayang Jin • Su Huang: Physics of petroleum Reservoirs, Petroleum Industry Press, Beijing, China 2017. P 71

saturation will never get to zero percent because some of the water will be trapped in some small pores and pore-throats. During hydrocarbon accumulation in the reservoir, water saturation may be reduced to a very small value, typically 10–40 %, till no more water can escape from the pores of the reservoir.

The water trapped in rock pores and becomes immobile called residual water. The saturation of this part of water is called residual water saturation. Sometimes it is also referred to as connate water saturation, primary water saturation, or irreducible saturation depending on different viewpoints from different investigators. [1]

At the end of the productive life of a reservoir, the oil that still remains in rock pores is referred to as residual oil. The fraction of pore volume occupied by residual oil in rocks is known as residual oil saturation. [2]

Residual oil saturation points to a value below which oil is no longer mobile within porous media. Residual oil saturation can be obtained from the core displacement in the laboratory. Knowledge of residual oil saturation

---

[1]Xuetao Hu • Shuyong Hu Fayang Jin • Su Huang: Physics of petroleum Reservoirs, Petroleum Industry Press, Beijing, China 2017. P 72

[2]Xuetao Hu • Shuyong Hu Fayang Jin • Su Huang: Physics of petroleum Reservoirs, Petroleum Industry Press, Beijing, China 2017. P 74

is of great interest to reservoir engineers as it can be used to estimate the ultimate recoverable reserves of oil reservoirs. Some studies prefer the term remaining oil saturation (ROS) in quantifying the oil left behind following the primary or a subsequent recovery. But the meanings of the two terms are essentially different.

Following the depletion of a typical reservoir based on natural drive mechanisms or secondary drive, a substantial portion of movable oil is usually left behind in the reservoir. The fraction of pore volume occupied by this movable oil left in reservoir rocks is known as remaining oil saturation. The remaining oil saturation encountered in the reservoir could be rather high. Reservoir engineers are interested to know the distribution of remaining oil saturations in a matured field, especially in the zones of bypassed oil for further recovery. The task requires multidisciplinary studies involving petrophysics, geology, geophysics, production, and reservoir simulation. [1]

Note that remaining oil usually refers to the oil remaining in reservoirs and being movable. It generally includes the oil either in

---

[1] Xuetao Hu • Shuyong Hu Fayang Jin • Su Huang: Physics of petroleum Reservoirs, Petroleum Industry Press, Beijing, China 2017. P 74

unswept dead oil area or in low-permeable layers/areas. The most important is that remaining oil can be recovered by secondary oil production method. Residual oil, however, means the immovable oil left in reservoirs after secondary oil recovery, and existing pores in extremely dispersed state. It is thus the target of tertiary oil recovery.

In the late of secondary oil recovery, an oil reservoir will implement appropriate improved or enhanced oil recovery (IOR or EOR) operations. Following a successful enhanced oil recovery operation in an oil reservoir, the remaining oil saturation is further reduced in the reservoir. For example, the study of a typical oil reservoir throughout its life cycle may lead to the following scenario. [1]

2.10. Critical gas saturation

Consider an oil reservoir in which no gas evolves out of liquid phase within the reservoir as long as the reservoir produces above the bubble point. When the reservoir pressure declines below the bubble point, gas evolves out of liquid phase but is not immediately mobile. Following the buildup of free gas saturation to a certain threshold value, referred to as critical gas saturation, the vapor phase begins to flow

---

[1] Xuetao Hu • Shuyong Hu Fayang Jin • Su Huang: Physics of petroleum Reservoirs, Petroleum Industry Press, Beijing, China 2017. P 74

toward the wellbore. Critical saturation is a term used in conjunction with increasing fluid saturation. [1]

Nearly all reservoirs are water bearing prior to hydrocarbon charge. As hydrocarbons migrate into a trap they displace the water from the reservoir, but not completely.

Water remains trapped in small pore throats and pore spaces. In 1942, Archie developed an equation describing the relationship between the electrical conductivity of reservoir rock and the properties of its pore system and pore fluids.

The relationship was based on a number of observations, firstly, that the conductivity (C_o) of a water-bearing formation sample is dependent primarily upon pore water conductivity (C_w) and porosity (Φ) distribution (as the rock matrix does not conduct electricity) such that

$$C_o = \phi^m C_w$$

The pore system is described by the volume fraction of pore space (the fractional porosity) and the shape of the pore space which

---

[1] Xuetao Hu • Shuyong Hu Fayang Jin • Su Huang: Physics of petroleum Reservoirs, Petroleum Industry Press, Beijing, China 2017. P 75

is represented by m, known as the cementation exponent. The cementation exponent describes the complexity of the pore system, that is how difficult it is for an electric current to find a path through the reservoir.

Secondly, it can be observed that as water is displaced by (non-conductive) oil in the pore system, the conductivity (C_t) of an oil-bearing reservoir sample decreases.

As the water saturation (S_w) reduces so does the electrical conductivity of the

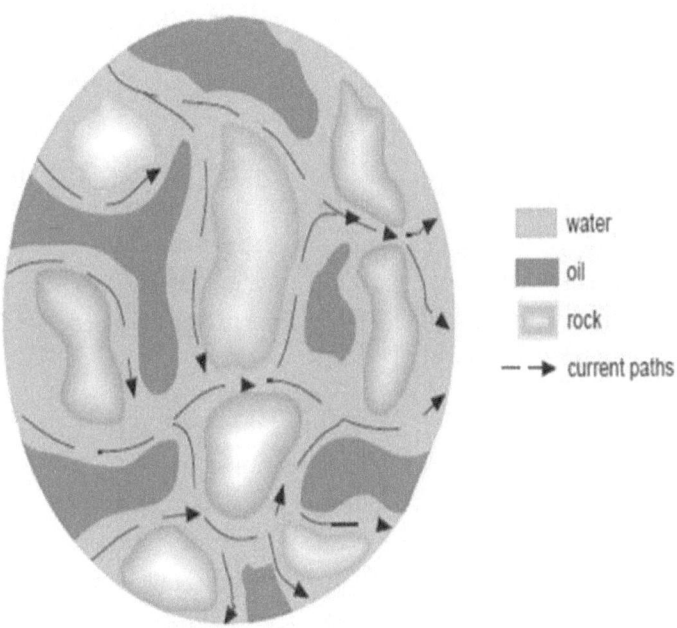

sample, such that

$$C_t = S_w^n \phi^m C_w$$

The volume fraction of water (S_w) and the saturation exponent n can be considered as expressing the increased difficulty experienced by an electrical current passing through a partially oil-filled sample. (Note: C_o is only a special case of C_t; when a reservoir sample is fully water bearing $C_o = C_t$.)

In practice, the logging tools are often used to measure the resistivity of the formation rather than the conductivity and therefore the equation above is more commonly inverted and expressed as

$$R_t = S_w^{-n} \phi^{-m} R_w$$

where R_t is the formation resistivity (ohmm), S_w the water saturation (fraction), f the porosity (fraction), R_w the water resistivity (ohmm), m the cementation exponent, and n the saturation exponent.

Formation resistivity is measured using a logging tool, porosity is determined from logs or cores and water resistivity can be determined from logs in water-bearing sections or measured on produced samples. In a large range of reservoirs, the saturation and cementation exponents can be taken as m = n = 2. The remaining unknown is the water saturation and the equation can be rearranged so that

$$S_w = \sqrt[n]{\frac{R_w}{\phi^m R_t}}$$ and hydrocarbon saturation (fraction) $S_h = 1 - S_w$

The most common method for measuring formation resistivity and hence determining hydrocarbon saturation is by logging with a resistivity tool such as the laterolog. The tool is designed to force electrical current through the formation

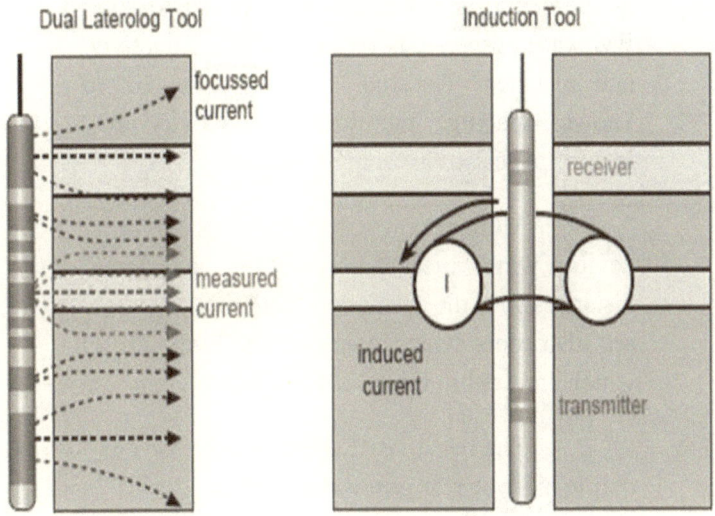

adjacent to the borehole and measure the potential difference across the volume investigated. With this information the formation resistivity can be calculated and output every foot as a resistivity log.

The laterolog tool needs a conductive environment to operate. Therefore, in oil-based mud (OBM) other types of tools are used. The most common is the induction log tool, based upon the principles of mine detection. A transmitting coil induces currents in the formation which in turn induce a current in the receiver coil.

The majority of FEWD resistivity tools use the electro-magnetic (EM) wave resistivity, as the signal is not affected by steel DCs. The EM wave response is a function of conductivity and distance. The tool has two receivers of known spacing, therefore conductivity (the inverse of resistivity) can be deduced.

More recent resistivity tools are array devices which measure resistivities at different distances into the formation. Additionally, there are also tools which measure resistivity in 3D which are used in thinly bedded rocks.

The resistivity log can also be used to define oil–water or gas–water contacts.

The Figure shows that the fluid contact can be defined as the point at which the resistivity begins to increase in the reservoir interval, inferring the presence of hydrocarbons above that point. [1]

3. Fossil Energy Reserves

Fossil energy reserves can be divided into inorganic reserves—as stored in all the elements in the form of binding energy at the nuclear level (exploited for energy supply in nuclear power plants in the form of fissile fuel, such as uranium and thorium)—and organic reserves, which is energy stored at molecular level in carbohydrates, the building blocks of the biosphere. Under highly particular conditions, after its life cycle, oxygen and water molecules are separated from the organic matter and expelled to the atmosphere while the hydrocarbon molecules remain trapped in deposits under the Earth's crust, undergoing millions of years of decomposition, heat and pressure forces. This process has given rise to the world's resources of oil and gas (created from water organisms buried under sea or river sediments) and coal (formed from the dead remains of trees, ferns and other plants).

In Table, an overview is given of the store of inorganic and organic fossil fuels on our planet at the end of 2008, divided into so-called reserves and resources. In this particular instance, with reserves we intend those sediments considered currently technologically

---

([1])Frank Jahn, Mark Cook and Mark Graham: HYDROCARBON EXPLORATION AND PRODUCTION. 2ND EDITION. Elsevier B.V. 2008. P 163: 166

and economically recoverable; resources are additionally demonstrated quantities that cannot be recovered at current prices with current technologies but might be recoverable in the future.

From the numbers for the store of fossil fuels and considering constant the current rate of extraction (2009 values), the so-called reserves-to-production ratio (or R/P ratio) can be calculated, which equates to the number of years it would take before the considered fuel reserves finish. This is not a realistic prospect, because as reserves deplete the production will be more and more difficult and laborious, but it is a helpful figure to get to grips with the availability of a particular fossil fuel.

The figures in Table are subject to change, not only because of depletion through consumption, but also as new reserves are discovered and extraction technology improves. Better geological knowledge on the state of sediments and more sophisticated methods of extraction allow also to squeeze extra quantities of e.g. oil and gas from sediments previously considered exhausted, converting what was intended as resources into winnable reserves.

New sediments of oil and gas continue to be discovered every year, but the quantities hidden under these successful exploratory drills is strategic information, capable of significantly perturbing the volatile market of these fuels (the petroleum industry is the world's biggest business). This gives rise to guesswork and speculative interpretation, which leads to contradictory information. As an example, two figures are reported displaying the quantity of oil discovered in new deposits year by year: Fig. 1.1a from a source that supports the belief that the supply of oil is peaking and will decline noticeably imminently; Fig. 1.1b from a source that generally advocates a sustained supply of oil for decades to come before depletion will become slowly noticeable. Both figures show consistent data regarding the production of oil, which is a relatively public datum, published in several freely accessible reviews, but the quantities of new oil discovered differ in trend as well as values.

In both figures, if we look at the trend over the last three-quarter century, we can clearly see that a decline has set in, and less new reserves are being unearthed.

In fact, more small sediments but less giant fields are being discovered, that account for by far the greatest share of global oil production. What we see in Fig. a, is that since 1981 new discoveries of oil do not keep up the pace of production, i.e. extraction. Furthermore, the gap between the two curves is increasing: the demand for oil has grown more or less continually, but new discoveries fail to reach even part of annual consumption. In Fig. b, the inflection between surplus and deficit of new oil found happens in 1988, with a gap that oscillates, but tends to remain constant.

In both figures above, the peaking curve of discoveries can be recognized, which can be approximated by the logistic curves for consumption of a finite commodity.

Whatever is the exact amount of recoverable fossil organic fuels, they are being consumed, and the products of their utilization (mainly through combustion) are being released from the mineral world back into the biosphere. As can be seen from these curves, the rate of consumption (corresponding to the time-derivative of the curves) peaks at a certain stage, after which the scarcity of the commodity will make its price increase, its availability less and its winning harder, so that consumption slows down and eventually dies out. It is therefore not to be feared that from one day to the next oil or gas or coal should finish. However, especially for oil, there is a severe chance of limitation on capacity taking hold, meaning that the demand cannot be satisfied fast enough by the fields in production.

For oil in particular, this pattern is known as the Hubbert curve (after the geophysicist who, in 1956, first predicted a short-term decline in oil production), though it is under debate when the peak will occur exactly. The figures of oil discovery above (Fig. a and b) already show a peak around the mid-sixties. One could infer from the curve and the latest updated figures for oil production that its stagnation is following, occurring in the last couple of years, but this could have been partly due to economic recession in the OECD countries in this period.

It is not excluded that there might be a new surge of discoveries as more remote and difficultly accessible sediments are explored: in the last decade two giant sediments were discovered in the Caspian Sea (the Kashagan field, discovered in 2000) and off the coast of São Paulo, Brazil (the Sugar Loaf field, discovered in 2007). Also, technology might arrive to the point where non-conventional fossil resources such as oil sands and oil shale can be recovered. But the rate of extraction will be lower as compared to the giant oil fields currently under exploitation and demand by that time will most probably be higher than today.

Furthermore, oil fields are concentrated in very few parts of the planet, which have already and could continue to give rise to political tension, especially as supply is put under pressure by increasing demand.

For the prospects of availability of gas and especially coal, things look more confident in terms of proved reserves and production rates.

However, though fossil fuel depletion remains an unresolved and topical issue, it is not only the decline of the amount of source material that needs to be carefully monitored. The curve in Fig. representing the products of consumption could have an even stronger, and more immediate effect on the planet's state and the intricate equilibrium of the biosphere in particular. [1]

Fuel type	Reserves (Gtoe)	R/P ratio (years)	Resources (Gtoe)
Crude oil	184	46	91
Natural gas	166	63	216
Total conventional hydrocarbons	350		307
Oil sands and extra heavy oil	39		190
Oil shale	–		119
Non-conventional natural gas[a]	4		2469
Total non-conv. hydrocarbons	43		2778
Anthracite and bituminous coal	356		9225
Sub-bituminous coal and lignite	218		1175
Total coal	574	119	10,400
Uranium[b]	17		139
Thorium[b]	22		24
Total Nuclear	39		163
Fossil fuels total	~1,000		~13,500

[a] Tight gas (24%), coal-bed gas (10%), aquifer gas (29%) and gas hydrates (37%)
[b] Assuming 1 t of Uranium (or Thorium) to yield 0.5 PJ ≈ 12 Mtoe (not considering nuclear breeder technology)

---

[1] Stephen J. McPhail • Viviana Cigolotti Angelo Moreno: Fuel Cells in the Waste-to-Energy Chain. Springer-Verlag London Limited 2012. P 5: 8

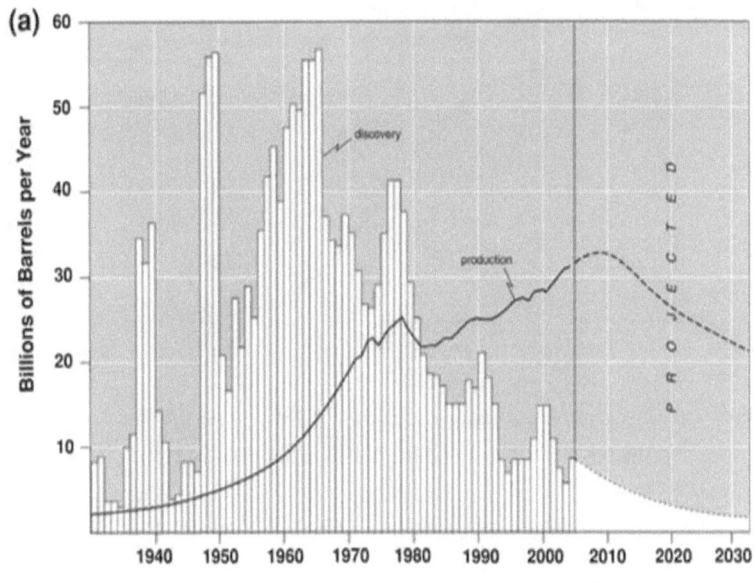

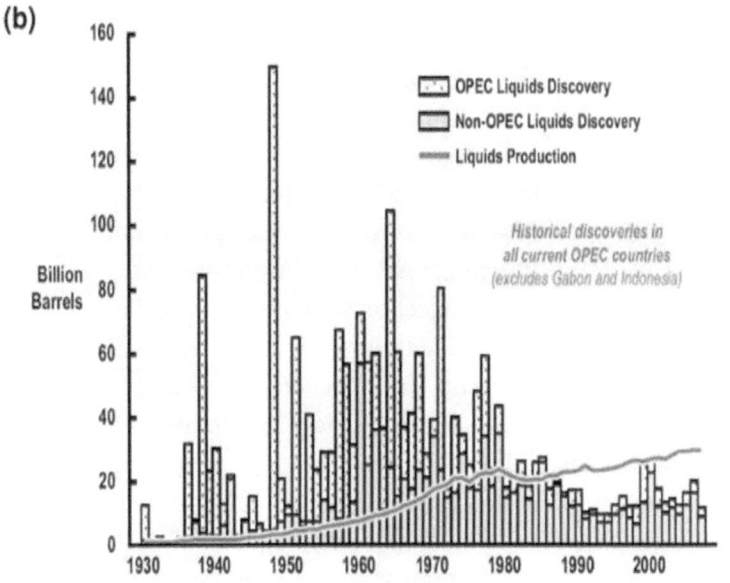

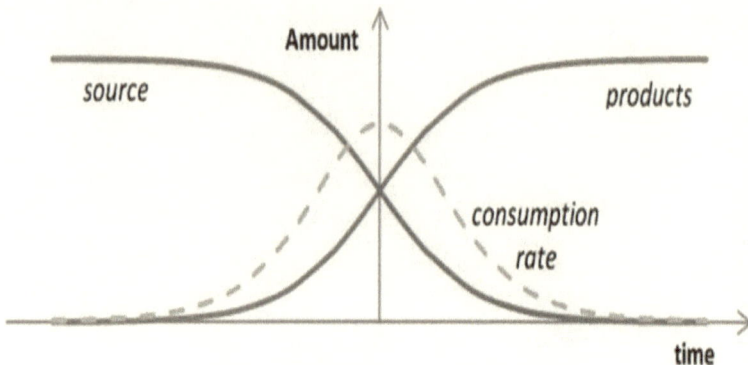

Although a relatively new idea in the context of climate change moderation, injecting CO2 into depleted oil and gas fields has been rehearsed for many years.

The prime purpose of these injections was the discarding off of "acid gas," a mixture of CO2, H2S and other byproducts of oil and gas exploitation and refining.

Basically, acid gas injection schemes take out CO2 and H2S from the oil or gas stream brought forth, compress and transport the gases via pipeline to an injection well, and re-inject the gases into a different formation for disposal. Proponents of acid gas injection postulate that these schemes affect in less environmental impact than substitutes for treating and disposing unwanted gases, where mostly CO2 constitutes up to 90 % of total injected volume. In past, depleted and producing reservoirs have demonstrated to be very reliable containers of both hydrocarbons and acid gases over time. [1]

3.1. Oil Reservoir

Oil reserves can generally be classified into cumulative production to date, proven reserves, and probable reserves. Proven reserves, however, are defined as the part of oil in place which can be produced under current economic and technical conditions without reasonable doubt. This includes all successfully tested areas as well as reserves that have been developed for production. At the end of 2010, world proven oil reserves were estimated to be 1.47 trillion barrels (bbl).

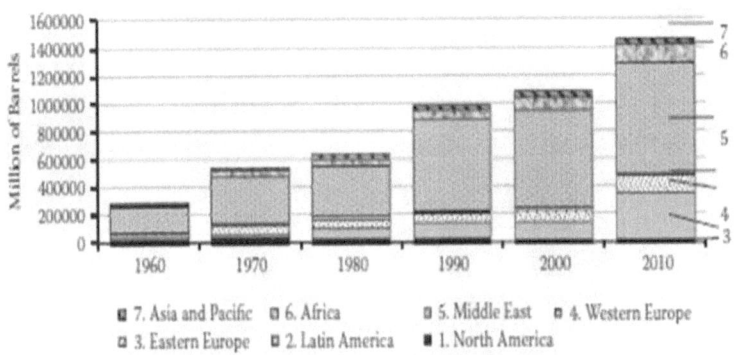

◨ 7. Asia and Pacific   ◻ 6. Africa   ◻ 5. Middle East   ◻ 4. Western Europe
◻ 3. Eastern Europe   ◻ 2. Latin America   ■ 1. North America

The Figure shows world distribution of oil proven reserves at the end of the year over the period 1960 to 2010. Until 1950 North

---

([1])V. Vishal • T.N. Singh: Geologic Carbon Sequestration. Springer International Publishing Switzerland 2016. P 12

America constituted the largest share of world oil proven reserves, but after 1960 other areas have emerged, such as the Middle East, which has the highest share. Its share rose to 65 percent of the world total by 1990 and continues to rise, while Latin America and Russia have followed, with 13 percent and 9 percent, respectively. The distribution of world oil proven reserves by OPEC nations compared to the rest of the world is presented in Figure. It shows the proven

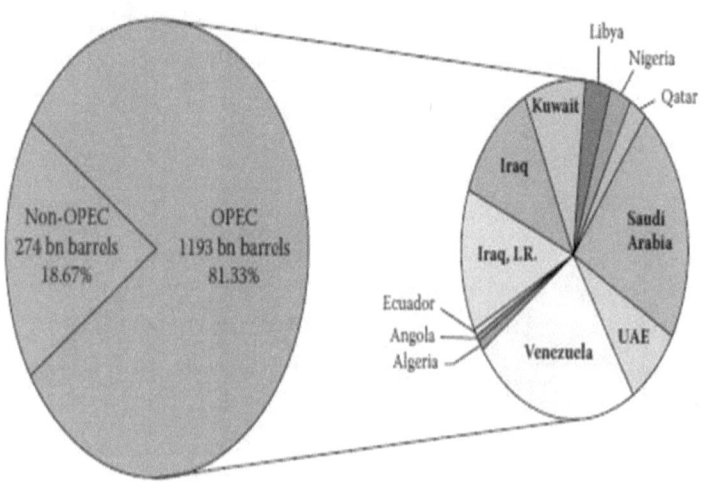

OPEC proven crude oil reserves, end 2010
(billions barrels)

Venezuela	296.50	24.8%	Iraq	143.10	12.0%	Libya	47.10	3.9%	Algeria	12.20	1.0%
Saudi Arabia	264.52	22.2%	Kuwait	101.50	8.5%	Nigeria	37.20	3.1%	Angola	9.50	0.8%
Iron, I.R.	151.17	12.7%	United Arab Emirates	97.80	8.2%	Qatar	25.38	2.1%	Ecuador	7.21	0.5%

oil reserves for countries at the end of 2010. Venezuela is at the top of the list, followed by Saudi Arabia, Iran, Iraq, and Kuwait. However, oil proven reserves for these countries have been revised upward lately. Changes in these estimates from year to year are due to changes in production levels, new discoveries, and extensions of the existing fields.

To measure the expected life of oil reserves, a ratio of proven reserves to annual production is calculated given certain assumptions. These assumptions include constant rate of production, stagnant oil demand, and no additional discoveries. For example, in the Gulf countries such as Saudi Arabia, the expected life of an oil reserve is around 90 years, where the average for the world is about 40 years. However, this ratio is changing over time as a result of changing oil prices and the state of technology. Rising oil prices in the 1970s and subsequent periods have stimulated more investment in exploration, even in relatively high-cost areas, which in turn has raised the proven reserves. This indicates that there is a positive correlation between oil prices and oil reserves. [1]

Hydrocarbons under initial reservoir temperature and pressure are predominatingly liquid hydrocarbons which are totally known as

---

[1]Hussein K. Abdel-Aal, Mohammed A. Alsahlawi: Petroleum Economics and Engineering. Third Edition. Taylor & Francis Group, LLC. 2014. P 4:6

crude oil. Crude oil in oil reservoirs is often referred to as light, intermediate, or heavy, which leads to the following classification of oil reservoirs. [1]

According to current estimates, 81.5% of the world's proven crude oil reserves are located in OPEC Member Countries, with the bulk of OPEC oil reserves in the Middle East, amounting to 65.5% of the OPEC total. OPEC Member Countries have made significant additions to their oil reserves in recent years, for example, by adopting best practices in the industry, realizing intensive explorations and enhanced recoveries. As a result, OPEC's proven oil reserves currently stand at 1,216.78 billion barrels. [2]

---

[1] Xuetao Hu • Shuyong Hu Fayang Jin • Su Huang: Physics of petroleum Reservoirs, Petroleum Industry Press, Beijing, China 2017. P 181
[2] http://www.opec.org/opec_web/en/index.htm

OPEC share of world crude oil reserves, 2016

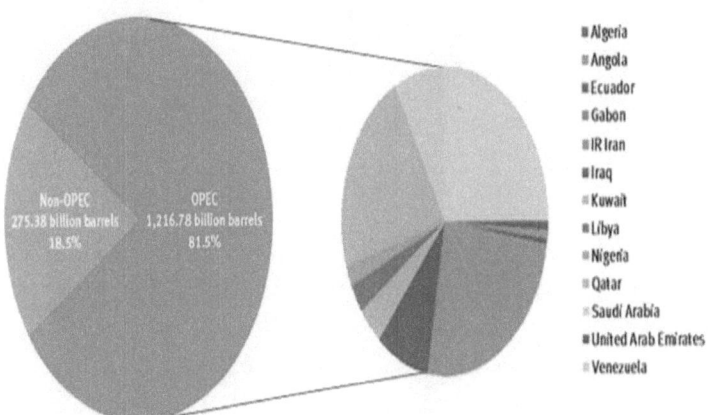

OPEC proven crude oil reserves, at end 2016 *(billion barrels, OPEC share)*

Venezuela	302.25	24.8%	Kuwait	101.50	8.3%	Qatar	25.24	2.1%	Gabon	2.00	0.2%
Saudi Arabia	266.21	21.9%	United Arab Emirates	97.80	8.0%	Algeria	12.20	1.0%			
IR Iran	157.20	12.9%	Libya	48.36	4.0%	Angola	9.52	0.8%			
Iraq	148.77	12.2%	Nigeria	37.45	3.1%	Ecuador	8.27	0.7%			

Source: OPEC Annual Statistical Bulletin 2017.

During the period 2007-2016, OPEC Member Countries added 279.0 billion barrels to their total proven crude oil reserves, a significant addition compared to other crude oil producers.

World proven crude oil reserves:
Cumulative production versus net additions, 2007-2016

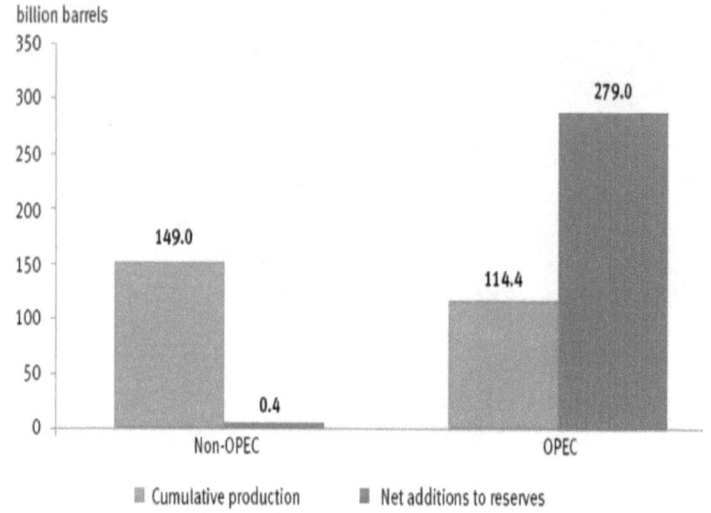

Source: OPEC Annual Statistical Bulletin 2017.

CO2 storage in depleted and producing oil reservoirs follows two objectives:

utilization of CO2 for enhanced oil recovery and permanent underground CO2 storage. CO2-EOR is a well-established technology that produces oil from the already-developed oilfields. The CO2-EOR process inevitably stores substantial volumes of CO2 in the subsurface formations, but the storage is not the prime benefit of the process. The storage aspect becomes an objective when anthropogenic CO2 is used instead of the natural CO2.

The synergy between the CO2-EOR and the anthropogenic CO2 storage provides an attractive alternative for the short-term mitigation of the greenhouse gas emissions.

From an environmental view point, a portion of the CO2 emissions from the oil production and consumption operations is offset via geological storage. From an economic viewpoint, a portion of the costs of CO2 capture, transport and injection processes are compensated by the incremental oil production. In the long-term, the EOR-storage projects have the following benefits.

1. Increase in the domestic oil production and energy security enhancement,

2. Promotion of the oilfield operators participation in the CO2 storage projects because of tax credits.

3. Expansion of the carbon capture, utilization and storage (CCUS) infrastructure, especially the pipeline network.

The EOR-storage projects need to overcome some major challenges before they become stablished as an industrial practice. A considerable impact on carbon emission reduction requires sustainable large-scale CO2 storage for decades. This requires that the pipeline network and infrastructure, subsurface uncertainties, regulatory framework, long-term liability, and public acceptance issues are all resolved.

The individual processes of CO2-EOR and CO2 storage have been addressed from different perspectives and we will cover the major aspects in this chapter. Our main focus, however, will be on the fundamental physical model of the EOR-storage process. [1]

3.1.1. Classifying Oil Reserves

Estimating oil reserves has proven the most controversial topic ever debated within the energy community, surpassing even the clash over nuclear power. The controversy harkens back to the very beginning of the twentieth century, grounded in opposite views about the threat posed by oil depletion. This means that we are now into the third generation of contenders. As the dispute unfolded, different streams of thought became progressively entrenched in separate organizations and spheres of influence. What is more, each side narrowly pigeonholed the other: Advocates of free markets were quipped "cornucopians" by associating the efficiency of spontaneous market adjustments in the regular supply of oil with the myth of endless abundance promised by the "horn of plenty" a cornucopia-like symbol of ancient

---

[1]V. Vishal • T.N. Singh: Geologic Carbon Sequestration. Springer International Publishing Switzerland 2016. P 185: 186

Greece; on the other hand, those warning against oil depletion risks were dubbed "doomsters," to buttress the parallelism between geo ecological mindful conjectures and obscure insights into the omens of doom.

From its very outset, the discussion was plagued by a profusion of classifications, definitions, and technical procedures and moreover impaired by the lack of binding international standards for the reporting of oil reserves. One important advance in this domain came from the common terminology established by the two most important professional organizations in the field, the Society of Petroleum Evaluation Engineers and the American Association of Petroleum Geologists (in 1997 and 2000, respectively). Beginning with the wider horizon of "petroleum initially in place," they propose the concept of "Ultimate Recoverable Resources" to account for the total amount of oil historically produced; the discovered reserves and the oil to be discovered in the future. Overall, the taxonomy encompasses several levels of forking from the existing mineral stock (resources), to the existing mineral stock which is both technically and economically exploitable (ultimate recoverable resources) over to the existing mineral stock technically and economically exploitable and that could be produced and marketed now (reserves). The point at which resources may be considered commercially exploitable sets the boundary for the new classification of "reserves." "Reserves," in turn, are further categorized according to three levels of confidence:

• Proven reserves (1P or P90) comprise the estimates for which there is a high degree of certainty of commercially recoverable oil given the prices and costs prevailing and under existing technical conditions. In probabilistic terms, P90 classification entails that after the accomplishment of detailed seismic analysis studies, core sampling, well-logging, and other tests, there should be at least a 90 % probability that the quantities actually recovered will equal or exceed the estimate.

• Probable reserves (2P or P50) comprise the estimates of more likely than not commercially recoverable reserves. P50 classification indicates that although unproven, geological, and engineering data suggest a probability equal to or above 50 % that the quantities actually recovered will equal or exceed the estimate.

In technical terms, this is, for instance, the case of "reserves in formations that appear productive based on well log characteristics but lack core data or definitive tests and which are clearly not analogous to producing or proven reservoirs in the area.

- Possible reserves (3P or P10) comprise the estimates of reserves less likely to be recovered than probable reserves. In probabilistic terms, P10 classification entails at least a 10 % chance that that the quantities actually recovered will equal or exceed the estimate. Generally speaking, the P10 classification is relevant whenever doubts about fluid, rock, and reservoir characteristics raise questions as regards commercial viability.

Until recently, much of the historical debate on oil depletion revolved around the amount of proven reserves (P1 or P90). In particular, this prevailed in conjectures in which uncertainties over the likelihood of finding untapped oil, favored the view that proven reserves might be nearer the total resource supply potential. With hindsight, these courses of action undersized the estimates in two different ways:

Firstly, by disregarding undiscovered resources; and secondly, by downsizing the discovered part. A proportion of the historical controversy over forthcoming scarcity or even depletion did, in effect, stem from equivocal interpretations about what this "proven" category meant. Only latterly did experts realize that the oil reported within this "lot" has been systematically less than forecast expectations.

The gap between the physical amount registered and the amount implicit in the main definition of "proven reserves" raised recurring misunderstandings regarding the factual situation faced by the industry. To make things worse, underreporting in field surveys, missing data in national oil surveys and politically adjusted data, amplified these statistical biases.

Field surveys are bottom-up inquiries that gather specific data about production in all the relevant wells/fields. Ultimately, their accuracy rests on figures and reports conveyed by oil firms and specialized information-scouting companies like IHS Energy (formerly Petroconsultants), which means that the dynamics of business interests leaves a most visible imprint on the final figures. From a micro perspective, what matters is the proven oil that may represent an asset for accounting purposes and quite commonly equated as the quantity of recoverable discovered oil that might be extracted through recourse to the infrastructure in place. The clout of business-accounting criteria over geological criteria is furthermore reinforced by regulatory preferences for conservative reserve statements, with a view to reducing commercial fraud. Nowhere has this tendency been more evident than in the USA, with regulations imposed by the US Securities and Exchange Commission (SEC) on Wall Street listed oil companies. The Commission has set strict rules for "proven" reserves to be booked, emphasizing the net present value evaluated by discounted cash flow, the business investment committed, as well as respective government approval. Even though there is an indirect connection with the physical reality of recoverable oil, the regulatory meaning of "proven" falls rather short of the geological yardstick. With short term accounting stocks replacing the broader geological principle of well/field life cycle, the problem of underreporting in the 1P category naturally accrued and particularly so in large fields.

At times, oil corporations also circumvent the need to update data by stating, in their annual reports, that the reserves have been more than replaced over the year in question whether by discoveries or by increases in the assessed recovery amounts in existing fields. Over the years, these practices stiffened and corporations moved into a reporting system in which reserves added through exploration just kept up with inventory maintenance. In so doing, they time and again postponed the revision of the real physical existing stock. However, it has been in the domain of national surveys that these missing data became an issue of major concern.

One possible explanation is that public agencies and national oil companies skip over the filling in of annual data for reasons similar to private corporations, namely that they find pointless to issue a statement whenever discoveries plus revisions match, to a greater or lesser extent, the production for the year in question.

Under such particular circumstances, the standard procedures for editors of benchmark reference publications such as the "Oil and Gas Journal," "World Oil," and "BP's Statistical Review of World Energy" are to reproduce the country's prior annual data. Owing to this, many authoritative sources publish proven reserve figures with no changes throughout consecutive years. Naturally, default reporting added further doubts as to the reliability of statistics, all the more so when half of oil-producing countries usually do not normally disclose changes in reserves.

Finally, we arrive at the political distortion of inquiries. Although politics has often interfered with the reporting of reserves, the most notorious case of statistical adjustment occurred in the Middle East oil states, during the 1980s, with proven reserves almost doubling overnight. Identified by the famous quip of "quota wars jumps," the boosting of 1P reserves somehow appeared an ingenious scheme for seizing higher production quotas while taking advantage of OPEC rules: Insofar as production shares were allocated on the basis of the size of reported proven reserves, the increase in declared amounts paved the way to grab a larger slice of the aggregate cartel output. Whether this was just a political expediency allowed by OPEC or also reflected something far more reaching, such as the end of the artificial measuring system established by the oil majors to restrict production, is still under discussion. In either case, the unfolding of events does appear driven by political agendas.

Systematic flaws in reporting, omissions of data, and untrustworthy time series deepened the gap between technical classifications and economic–political constraints.

In the end, factors other than geological probability and economic certainty combined to undermine the concept of "proven reserves." Regardless of the clear-cut framing of categories, formal definitions struck into the diversity of interests, practices, agents, and regulations. In this context, drawing upon so imperfect a construct to ascertain how much recoverable oil remained in the planet seemed of little help. Yet, experts and public opinion were utterly obsessed with the depletion of proven reserves in 1910, and all over again in the 1970s, sometimes taking the resource potential at face value. A very significant turnaround occurred only at the dawn of the twenty-first century, with the shift of the debate toward 2P—probable reserves.

To fully understand this changeover, it is necessary to realize that, with the passage of time, probable reserves (2P) are converted into proven reserves (1P).

The sliding process results from the advance of field exploration and the inherent mastering of geological conditions, improvements in extraction technologies, market changes, and changes in reporting practices. Basically, better knowledge and better technology prompts an upward revision of the recoverable reserves, a process dubbed "reserves growth." In practical terms, the framing of the debate on oil depletion over the boundaries of 2P entailed the recognition of upcoming proven reserves growth as the closest gauge to assess the volumes of accessible oil in the ground. Strange as it may sound, "probable" turned out to be more accurate than "certain": not only did 2P reflect the empirical rule of thumb of "more likely than not," but it smoothly slipped the leash of interference by regulatory organizations, business interests, companies, and governments. Relatively insulated from the political and economic decision sphere, 2P data showed, moreover, high responsiveness to geological breakthroughs and the potential to provide the best estimate for each field's ultimately recoverable reserves (URR).

The final and obvious outcome of the switch toward the probable reserves category derives from the extension of the life span of stocks along with the view that the depletion path had no bearing on a deterministic time limit. The ensuing pages depict the historical contexts of the debate on depletion from the 1910s to the present- day, pinpointing arguments, methods, and outcomes. [1]

3.1.2. Volatile Oil Reservoir

Hydrocarbons are initially found in the liquid phase in oil reservoirs. However, an oil reservoir may be discovered with an overlying gas cap when the initial reservoir pressure is lower than the bubble point of the crude oil. When the reservoir pressure declines, relatively light-hydrocarbon components can evolve out of the liquid phase in large quantities. Volatile crude is typically light to dark amber color. The API gravity of typical volatile oils is relatively high, 38° or above (relative density 0.83 or lower than 0.83). Crude oil with an API gravity of 45° or greater (relative density 0.80 or lower than 0.80) is referred to as near-critical oil, implying the location of the system near the critical point on the p–T phase diagram and the abundance of highly volatile hydrocarbons. This kind of reservoir is called near-critical oil reservoir. This kind of reservoir has been discovered in Jilin, Zhongyuan and western

---

[1] Nuno Luis Madureira: Key Concepts in Energy. Springer International Publishing Switzerland 2014. P 101: 105

region of China, North Sea of United Kingdom, and eastern region of United States.

3.1.3. Black Oil Reservoir

The term "black oil" is frequently cited in reservoir simulation studies as various volatile components are collectively considered to be single gas phase due to the relatively low volatility of crude encountered in many reservoirs. It is used here to categorize oil reservoirs that fall in between the volatile and heavy oil reservoirs in terms of the specific gravity of crude. The gravity range of typical crude would be 38°–22.3°API (relative density: 0.83–0.92) (approximately). Abundance of intermediate hydrocarbons is the typical characteristic of black oils. The color of black oils is variable, from green to black. [1]

For both volatile oil and black oil, the initial reservoir temperature is below the critical point, and the fluid is therefore a liquid in the reservoir. As the pressure drops, the bubble point is eventually reached, and the first bubble of gas is released from the liquid. The composition of this gas will be made up of the more volatile components of the mixture. Both volatile oils and black oils will liberate gas in the separators, whose conditions of pressure and

---

[1]Xuetao Hu • Shuyong Hu Fayang Jin • Su Huang: Physics of petroleum Reservoirs, Petroleum Industry Press, Beijing, China 2017. P 181: 182

temperature are well inside the two-phase envelope.

A volatile oil contains a relatively large fraction of lighter and intermediate components which vaporize easily. With a small drop in pressure below the bubble point, the relative amount of liquid to gas in the two-phase mixture drops rapidly, as shown in the phase diagram by the wide spacing of the iso-vol lines. At reservoir pressures below the bubble point, gas is released in the reservoir, and is known as solution gas, since above the bubble point this gas was contained in solution.

Some of this liberated gas will flow towards the producing wells, whilst some will remain in the reservoir and migrate towards the crest of the structure to form a secondary gas cap.

Black oils are a common category of reservoir fluids, and are similar to volatile oils in behavior, except that they contain a lower fraction of volatile components and therefore require a much larger pressure drop below the bubble point before significant volumes of gas are released from solution. This is reflected by the position of the iso-vol lines in the phase diagram, where the lines of low liquid percentage are grouped around the dew point line.

Volatile oils are known as high shrinkage oils because they liberate relatively large amounts of gas either in the reservoir or the separators, leaving relatively smaller amounts of stabilized oil compared to black oils (also called low shrinkage oils).

When the pressure of a volatile oil or black oil reservoir is above the bubble point, we refer to the oil as undersaturated. When the pressure is at the bubble point we refer to it as saturated oil, since if any more gas were added to the system it could not be dissolved in the oil. The bubble point is therefore the saturation pressure for the reservoir fluid.

An oil reservoir which exists at initial conditions with an overlying gas cap must by definition be at the bubble point pressure at the interface between the gas and the oil, the gas–oil contact (GOC). Gas existing in an initial gas cap is called free gas, whilst the gas in solution in the oil is called dissolved or solution gas. [1]

---

[1] Frank Jahn, Mark Cook and Mark Graham: HYDROCARBON EXPLORATION AND PRODUCTION. 2ND EDITION. Elsevier B.V. 2008. P 122: 123

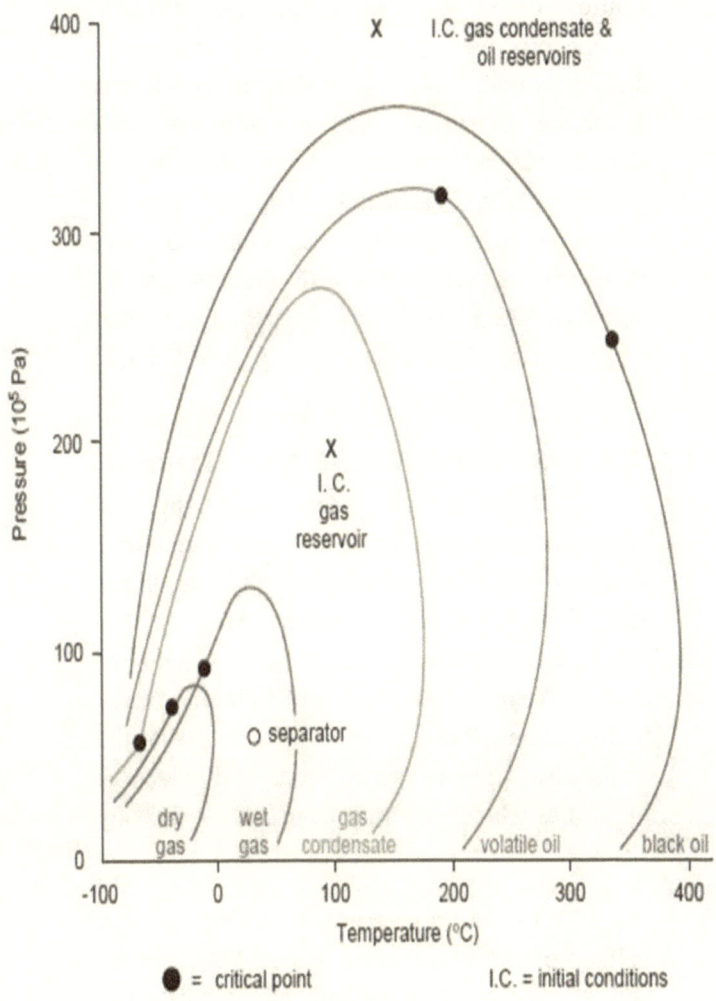

3.1.4. Heavy Oil Reservoir

Heavy and extra-heavy oil reservoirs exhibit a dominance of heavier hydrocarbons in the composition of crude. According to the standard made at 11th World Petroleum

Conference in London, 1983, viscous crude (heavy oil) means the oil having a relative density of 0.934–1.00 under standard conditions at surface. The viscosity of degassed heavy oils at reservoir temperature is about 100 mPa s or greater, even exceeding 10,000 mPa s sometimes. At present, according to API classification, reservoirs with crude's gravity less than 22.3° (relative density higher than 0.92) are considered to be heavy oil reservoirs. [1]

3.1.5. CRUDE CONDITIONING AND STORAGE

Hydrocarbon gases and light and heavy hydrocarbon liquids are all present in a single homogeneous phase under pressure in the formation before it is drilled. After this is released from the formation, components of crude oil separate into layers of light and heavy hydrocarbons. Raw crude oil collected from the wells also contains sand, mud, and water as impurities which may vary from 20% to 30% by volume.

Hence, raw crude is collected in a battery of treatment tanks where both storage and treatment of crude oil are carried out. Treatment steps involve gravity settling and removal of sand and water followed by chemical

---

([1])Xuetao Hu • Shuyong Hu Fayang Jin • Su Huang: Physics of petroleum Reservoirs, Petroleum Industry Press, Beijing, China 2017. P 182

treatment to remove emulsified water and, finally, to a crude conditioning unit. Gases lighter than propane have a tendency to escape, whereas propane and heavier gases are found dissolved in crude oil at atmospheric pressure. Proper mixing and repeated heating above room temperature (usually 45°C–50°C at low pressure and up to 90°C at a pressure of 2–3 atm) followed by cooling to storage temperature can increase the dissolution of gases and homogenize the layers of light and heavy liquid hydrocarbons.

Segregated wax in crude oil may choke the pipeline and pumping equipment due to deposition. Heating of crude with a mixing facility reduces segregation of wax by making it uniformly distributed in the bulk and thus it can be stored and transported without risk of deposition for many hours at room temperature or lower temperature above the *pour point*. Asphaltic and heavy hydrocarbons with high viscosity are also mixed up with wax and other hydrocarbon components during the heating and cooling cycle, making them less viscous. Heating can be

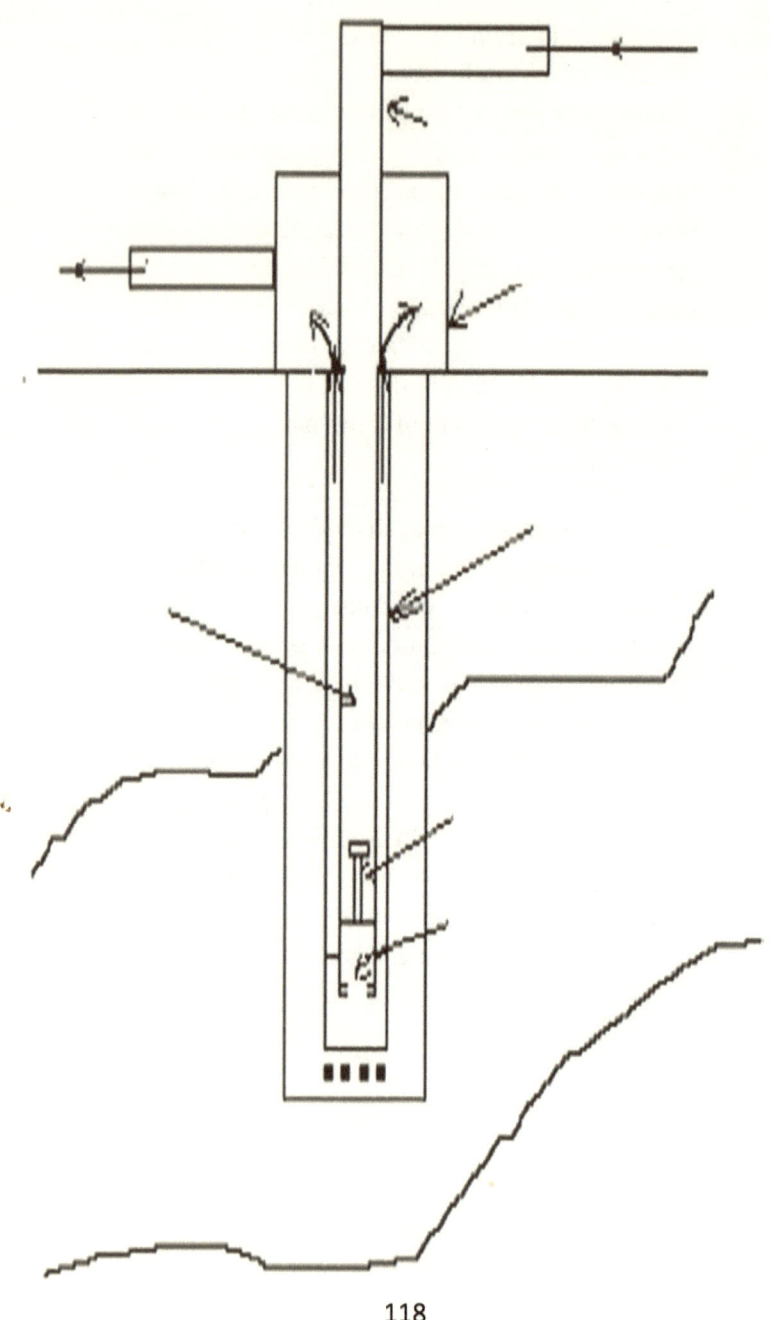

provided by a steam coil in the storage vessel with mechanical mixers, and cooling is done in another vessel with cooling coils in which refrigerants may be the vaporizing hydrocarbon gas or other liquids. Heating and cooling vessels are connected in sequence. Conditioning of crude oil can also be done by heating and cooling in sequence in pipe coils at the required temperatures. Mixing is enhanced for high velocity in the pipe coils. This type of conditioning method reduces the cost of storage and loss of gases. Conditioning may also be used for mixing oil and gases from various wells in the desired proportion to meet the desired quality. Water and slop (oil and water mixture) from the treatment unit is also treated in the battery before recycling to wells. [1]

3.1.6. Tar Sand

Tar sands, also variously called oil sands or bituminous sands, are loose-to-consolidated sandstone or a porous carbonate rock, impregnated with bitumen. Bitumen is a high boiling asphaltic material with an extremely high viscosity that is immobile under reservoir conditions and vastly different to conventional petroleum. On an international note, the bitumen in tar sand deposits represents a potentially large supply of energy. However, many of the

---

[1]Uttam Ray Chaudhuri: Fundamentals of Petroleum and Petrochemical Engineering. Taylor and Francis Group. 2011. P 19: 20

reserves are available only with some difficulty and that optional refinery scenarios will be necessary for conversion of these materials to liquid products because of the substantial differences in character between conventional petroleum and tar sand bitumen.

Because of the diversity of available information and the continuing attempts to delineate the various world tar sand deposits, it is virtually impossible to present accurate numbers that reflect the extent of the reserves in terms of the barrel unit. Indeed, investigations into the extent of many of the world's deposits are continuing at such a rate that the numbers vary from 1 year to the next. Accordingly, the data quoted here must be recognized as approximate with the potential of being quite different at the time of publication. [1]

The bitumen in tar sand deposits is estimated to be at least, 1.7 trillion barrels (1.7 * 10^{12} barrels) in the Canadian Athabasca tar sand deposits and 1.8 trillion barrels (1.8 * 10^{12} barrels) in the Venezuelan Orinoco tar sand deposits, compared to 1.75 trillion barrels (1.3 * 10^{12} barrels) of conventional oil worldwide, most of it in Saudi Arabia and other Middle Eastern countries. Eighty-one percent of the

---

[1] Xuetao Hu • Shuyong Hu Fayang Jin • Su Huang: Physics of petroleum Reservoirs, Petroleum Industry Press, Beijing, China 2017. P 183: 184

world's known recoverable bitumen is in the Athabasca tar sands of Alberta, Canada. In addition, bitumen reserves under active development are also included in the official estimate of crude oil reserves for Canada.

In spite of the high estimations of the reserves of bitumen, the two conditions of vital concern for the economic development of tar sand deposits are the concentration of the resource, or the percent bitumen saturation, and its accessibility, usually measured by the overburden thickness. Recovery methods are based either on mining combined with some further processing or operation on the oil sands in situ. The mining methods are applicable to shallow deposits, characterized by an overburden ratio (i.e., overburden depth to thickness of tar sand deposit). For example, indications are that for the Athabasca deposit, no more than 15 % of the in-place deposit is available within current concepts of the economics and technology of open-pit mining; this 10 % portion may be considered as the proven reserves of bitumen in the deposit. [1]

---

[1]Xuetao Hu • Shuyong Hu Fayang Jin • Su Huang: Physics of petroleum Reservoirs, Petroleum Industry Press, Beijing, China 2017. P 184: 185

3.1.7. Distribution of Unconventional Crude Oils

There are vast deposits of unconventional crude oils located in more than 30 countries around the World. Their estimated reserves are more than 6 trillion barrels of oil, accounting for about 70 % of total World oil reserves The origin of these deposits is the microbial biodegradation of light oils over millions of years, which modifies the molecular composition and physical properties of crude oil: the percentage of low molecular weight compounds, saturates and aromatic fractions is reduced, whereas the concentration of resins, asphaltenes and sulfur is increased, leading to high oil densities and viscosities and to a decrease in the quality of the oil. [1]

The largest extra-heavy crude oil reservoir in the World is the Orinoco Oil Belt, located in the north of the Orinoco River in Venezuela. In October 2009, the United States Geological Survey estimated that it contained 513 billion barrels of recoverable oil, making this area the World's first recoverable oil deposit, ahead of Saudi Arabia, which estimated oil reserves are 240 billion barrels. Other important extra-heavy oil reservoirs are the

---

[1]Kirsten Heimann • Obulisamy Parthiba Karthikeyan Subramanian Senthilkannan Muthu: Biodegradation and Bioconversion of Hydrocarbons. Springer Science+Business Media Singapore 2017. P 340: 341

Athabasca Oil Sands (Alberta, Canada), which oil reserves considered to be technically recoverable are estimated to be 280–300 billion barrels. In Mexico, it is estimated that 61.9 %of the oil reserves correspond to heavy or extra-heavy crudes. In China, heavy crude oil reserves are also significant (1.64 billion tons), and account for 20 % of the Chinese oil reserves. [1]

The increasing energy demand in the upcoming years will make necessary the exploitation of unconventional crude oil reserves, including heavy and extra-heavy crude oils. However, their exploitation requires the application of special techniques in order to facilitate their recovery, transportation and refining. The chemical and thermal methods commonly used are expensive and environmentally hazardous, which resulted in an increased interest in the application of biological treatments to reduce the viscosity and density of unconventional crude oils, as a cheaper and environmentally friendly alternative or as a complementary technology. The bioconversion of crude oil is a process where heavy oil fractions are converted into lighter ones due to the action of microorganisms, resulting in an enrichment in lighter hydrocarbons, and

---

[1]Kirsten Heimann • Obulisamy Parthiba Karthikeyan Subramanian Senthilkannan Muthu: Biodegradation and Bioconversion of Hydrocarbons. Springer Science+Business Media Singapore 2017. P 341

consequently, a reduction in oil viscosity and an increase in its mobility, which contributes to increase oil recovery and, at the same time, the quality of the oil. The available research shows that biological upgrading of crude oil, at least to some extent, is a technically feasible process that may be at least a feasible complementary process, if not a replacement for conventional upgrading techniques. However, its application at an industrial level has not been achieved yet, and more research will be necessary to implement this promising technology. [1]

3.2. Gas Reservoir

Natural gas is the gaseous mixture associated with petroleum reservoirs and is predominantly methane but does contain other combustible hydrocarbon compounds as well as nonhydrocarbon compounds. In fact, associated natural gas is believe d to be the most economical form of ethane. Natural gas has no distinct odor and the main use is for fuel, but it can also be used to make chemicals and liquefied petroleum gas (LPG).

The gas occurs in the porous rock of the earth' s crust either alone or with accumulations of petroleum. In the latter case, the gas forms the gas cap, which is the mass of

---

[1]Kirsten Heimann • Obulisamy Parthiba Karthikeyan Subramanian Senthilkannan Muthu: Biodegradation and Bioconversion of Hydrocarbons. Springer Science+Business Media Singapore 2017. P 348

gas trapped between the liquid petroleum and the impervious cap rock of the petroleum reservoir. When the pressure in the reservoir is sufficiently high, the natural gas may be dissolved in the petroleum and is released upon penetration of the reservoir as a result of drilling operations.

There are several general definitions that have been applied to natural gas. Thus, lean gas is gas in which methane is the major constituent. Wet gas contains considerable amounts of the higher molecular weight hydrocarbons. Sour gas contains hydrogen sulfide, whereas sweet gas contains very little, if any, hydrogen sulfide. Residue gas is natural gas from which the higher molecular weight hydrocarbons have been extracted and casing head gas is derived from petroleum but is separated at the separation facility at the wellhead.

To further define the terms dry and wet in quantitative measures, the term dry natural gas indicates that there is less than 0.1-gallon (1 (US) gallon = 264.2 m^3) of gasoline vapor (higher molecular weight paraffins) per 1000 ft^3 (1 ft^3 = 0.028 m^3). The term wet natural gas indicates that there are such paraffins present in the gas, in fact more than 0.1 gal=1000 ft^3.

Associated or dissolved natural gas occurs either as free gas or as gas in solution in the petroleum. Gas that occurs as a solution in the petroleum is dissolved gas, whereas the gas that exists in contact with the petroleum (gas cap) is associated gas.

Other components such as carbon dioxide (CO_2), hydrogen sulfide (H_2S), mercaptans (thiols; R–SH), as well as trace amounts of other constituents, may also be present. Thus, there is no single composition of components that might be termed typical natural gas.

Methane and ethane constitute the bulk of the combustible components; carbon dioxide (CO_2) and nitrogen (N_2) are the major noncombustible (inert) components.

Some natural gas wells also produce helium, which can occur in commercial quantities; nitrogen and carbon dioxide are also found in some natural gases. Gas is usually separated at as high a pressure as possible, reducing compression costs when the gas is to be used for gas lift or delivered to a pipeline. After gas removal, lighter hydrocarbons and hydrogen sulfide are removed as necessary to obtain a crude oil of suitable vapor pressure for transport yet retaining most of the natural gasoline constituents.

In addition to composition and thermal content (Btu=scft, Btu=ft^3), natural gas can also be characterized on the basis of the mode of the natural gas found in reservoirs where there is no or at best only minimal amounts of crude oil.

Thus, there is nonassociated natural gas, which is found in reservoirs in which there is no, or at best only minimal amounts of, crude oil. Nonassociated gas is usually richer in methane but is markedly leaner in terms of the higher molecular weight hydrocarbons and condensate.

Conversely, there is also associated natural gas (dissolved natural gas) which occurs either as free gas or as gas in solution in the crude oil. Gas that occurs as a solution with the crude petroleum is dissolved gas, whereas the gas that exists in contact with the crude petroleum (gas cap) is associated gas. Associated gas is usually leaner in methane than the nonassociated gas but is richer in the higher molecular weight constituents.

Another product is gas condensate, which contains relatively high amounts of the higher molecular weight liquid hydrocarbons. These hydrocarbons may occur in the gas phase in the reservoir.

The most preferred type of natural gas is the nonassociated gas. Such gas can be produced at high pressure, whereas associated, or dissolved, gas must be separated from petroleum at lower separator pressures, which usually involves increased expenditure for compression.

Thus, it is not surprising that such gas (under conditions that are not economically favorable) is often flared or vented.

The nonhydrocarbon constituents of natural gas can be classified as two types of materials:

1. Diluents, such as nitrogen, carbon dioxide, and water vapors

2. Contaminants, such as hydrogen sulfide or other sulfur compounds

The diluents are noncombustible gases that reduce the heating value of the gas and are on occasion used as fillers when it is necessary to reduce the heat content of the gas. On the other hand, the contaminants are detrimental to production and transportation equipment in addition to being obnoxious pollutants. Thus, the primary reason for gas processing is to remove the unwanted constituents of natural gas.

The major diluents or contaminants of natural gas are

1. Acid gas, which is predominantly hydrogen sulfide although carbon dioxide does occur to a lesser extent

2. Water, which includes all entrained free water or water in condensed forms

3. Liquids in the gas, such as higher boiling hydrocarbons as well as pump lubricating oil, scrubber oil, and, on occasion, methanol

4. Any solid matter that may be present, such as fine silica (sand) and scaling from the pipe

As with petroleum, natural gas from different wells varies widely in composition and analyses and the proportion of nonhydrocarbon constituents can vary over a very wide range. Thus, a particular natural gas field could require production, processing, and handling protocols different from those used for gas from another field.

Liquefied petroleum gas is composed of propane (C_3H_8), butanes (C_4H_{10}), or mixtures thereof, small amounts of ethane (C_2H_6) and pentane (C_5H_{12}) may also be present as impurities. On the other hand, natural gasoline (like refinery gasoline) consists mostly of pentane (C_5H_{12}) and higher molecular weight hydrocarbons.

The term natural gasoline has also on occasion in the gas industry been applied to mixtures of LPG, pentanes, and higher molecular weight hydrocarbons. Caution should be taken not to confuse natural gasoline with the term straight-run gasoline (often also incorrectly referred to as natural gasoline), which is the gasoline distilled unchanged from petroleum.

The proven reserves of natural gas are in excess of 3600 trillion cubic feet (1 Tcf = 1 * 10 ^{12}). Approximately 300 Tcf exist in the United States and Canada. It should also be remembered that the total gas resource base (like any fossil fuel or miner al resource base) is dictated by econ omics. Therefore, when resource da ta are quoted, some attention must be given to the cost of recovering those resources. Most important, the economics must also include a cost factor that reflects the willingness to secure total, or a specific degree of, energy independence. [1]

---

[1]James G. Speight: The Chemistry and Technology of Petroleum. FOURTH EDITION. Taylor & Francis Group, LLC. 2007. P 108:110

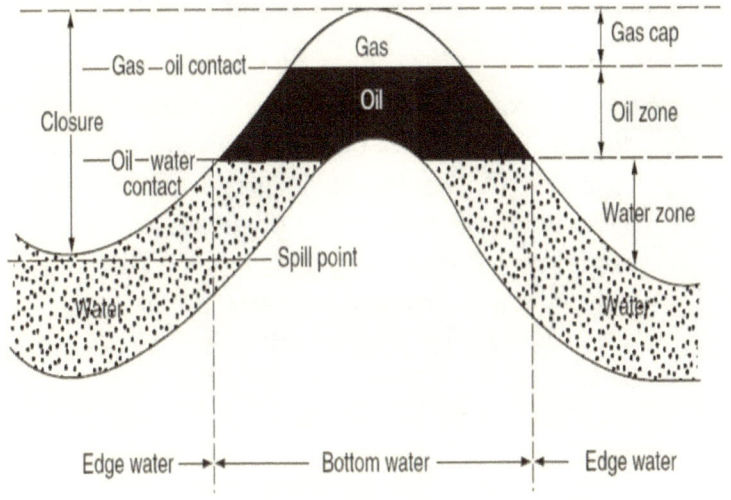

In addition to the natural gas found in petroleum reservoirs, there are also those reservoirs in which natural gas may be the sole occupant. The principal constituent of natural gas is methane, but other hydrocarbons, such as ethane, propane, and butane, may also be present.

Carbon dioxide is also a common constituent of natural gas. Trace amounts of rare gases, such as helium, may also occur, and certain natural gas reservoirs are a source of these rare gases. Just as petroleum can vary in composition, so can natural gas. Differences in natural gas composition occur between different reservoirs, and two wells in the same field may also yield gaseous products that are different in composition. [1]

Natural hydrate deposits can be divided into four classes. Class 1 deposits are composed of two layers: an underlying two-phase fluid zone with mobile (free) gas, and an overlying hydrate-bearing layer (HBL) containing water and hydrate (Class 1 W) or gas and hydrate (Class 1G). In Class 1 deposits, the bottom of the hydrate stability zone (HSZ) coincides with the bottom of the HBL.

Class 2 deposits comprise two zones: the HBL overlying a mobile water zone. Class 3 deposits are composed of a single zone, the HBL. And this type of deposit is characterized by the absence of an underlying zone of mobile fluids. In Class 2 and 3 deposits, the entire hydrate interval may be at or within the HSZ. Class 4 deposits involve disperse, low-saturation accumulations in marine geologic media that are not bounded by confining strata and can extend over large areas. Within these four classes, Class 1 reservoirs are thought to be the easiest and probably the first type of hydrate reservoir to be produced. Although most of the seafloor lies within the low-temperature and high-pressure conditions necessary for hydrate formation,

---

[1] James G. Speight: The Chemistry and Technology of Petroleum. FOURTH EDITION. Taylor & Francis Group, LLC. 2007. P 54

hydrates are generally found in sediments along continental margins, where adequate supplies of biogenic gases are available.

Technologies for recovering methane (CH4) from gas hydrates reservoirs are very challenging and still under development. The general concept of producing natural gas from geologic deposits of gas hydrates is to alter the reservoir environment (i.e., temperature or pressure) so that the gas hydrates transit from being thermodynamically stable to unstable. The thermodynamic stability of gas hydrates is dependent upon the temperature and pressure of guest molecules as well as aqueous solute concentrations. Accordingly, the three most practical methods for gas hydrates harvesting are: (1) depressurization, in which the pressure of an adjacent gas phase or water phase is reduced to trigger gas hydrates decomposition; (2) thermal stimulation, in which an external source of energy is provided to increase the temperature; and (3) inhibitor injection, in which methanol or a combination of inhibitors is used to de-equilibrate the system by raising the aqueous solute concentration. An alternative approach is to reduce the partial pressure of the guest molecule by introducing a substitute guest molecule, such as carbon dioxide. For example, introducing carbon dioxide into geologic media filled with methane hydrate results in the displacement of methane with carbon dioxide as a guest molecule without dissociating the hydrate. Among these methods, thermal stimulation models are produced from laboratories. Depressurization, on the other hand, has been the method used in the field production such as in the Messoyakha field, USSR. [1]

As the production continues, reservoir pressure declines and causes a reduction in the petroleum production rate. In these cases, using artificial lift methods such as gas lift is inevitable. Gas lift helps the reservoir which is able to drive oil to the well bottom but not to the surface to produce in an economic rate. In this method, gas is injected to the well, dissolves in oil and decreases the head pressure in the well. Thus, the pressure difference between the bottom hole and the well head increases and causes an increment in oil production. [2]

In the formulation of every optimization problem, first a fitness function should be defined. The fitness function catches some inputs (here gas injection rate (q_{gi}) of different wells) and returns the output. Output can be a single value or an array of values (multi

---

[1] Congrui Jin • Gianluca Cusatis: New Frontiers in Oil and Gas Exploration. Springer International Publishing Switzerland 2016. P 52
[2] Ehsan Khamehchi • Mohammad Reza Mahdiani: Gas Allocation Optimization Methods in Artificial Gas Lift. 2017. P 1

objective). The purpose of the optimizer is to maximize or minimize the output. The relation between the outputs and inputs is called the fitness or objective function. In addition, it is very common for every optimization problem to have some constraints. The optimizer should find a point which minimizes or maximizes the output while satisfying all constraints.

The increment of the oil depends on many factors such as gas injection rate and reservoir and well properties. In addition, greater oil production does not necessarily mean more profit, and the cost of production, such as the cost of the compressors, should be considered. Usually, in gas allocation most of the involved parameters cannot be changed due to previous design and installation and only the gas injection rates remain as changeable, and thus the maximum profit corresponds to the maximum oil production. Gas allocation optimization is a process of finding the best allocation which causes the maximum profit. The Figure shows a schematic of the gas allocation process.

This optimization based on the performance of each well, assigns some gas to each well in which the total profit of all wells is maximized and also some constraints are satisfied.

First, the formulation of the problem and different methods (such as the building the proxy models) will be reviewed and the advantages and disadvantages of each method will be surveyed. Afterwards, different constraints that can be considered in this problem will be discussed and finally the optimization algorithms and their efficiency will be reviewed. [1]

---

[1] Ehsan Khamehchi • Mohammad Reza Mahdiani: Gas Allocation Optimization Methods in Artificial Gas Lift. 2017. P 2: 3

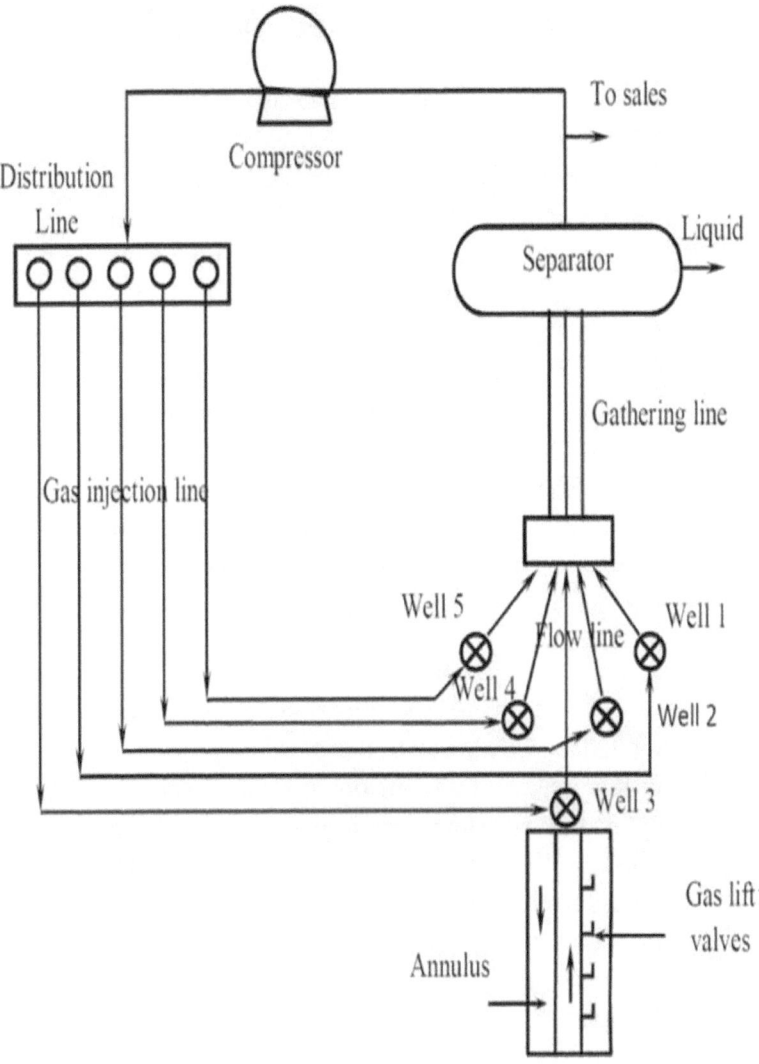

When just one well is considered, the amount of injected gas has an important effect on net present value. Thus, more oil production does not necessarily mean more profit because of the cost of gas injection such as the compressor On the other hand, usually a compressor with constant power is installed and all its capacity is used. Thus, its cost is fixed. Altering the share of different wells would not change other capital costs, and thus the net present value is proportional to the production rate. So in many problems, the cumulative production rate is considered as the value of fitness function and the optimizer tries to maximize it. However, some other parameters such as time are still important in the net present value. The back payment is very dominant in calculations and as the pressure of the reservoir decreases, the back payment at different times is not the same. It is clear that for considering this there is a need for the integrated model. [1]

If in a gas allocation there is no limitation, the allocation means nothing. In fact, in this situation, gas lift optimization means to optimize well parameters in design stages for a single well. In a single well, by increasing the injection rate the production increases but if it increases too high, production decreases because of some other interfering parameters such as friction.

---

[1]Ehsan Khamehchi • Mohammad Reza Mahdiani: Gas Allocation Optimization Methods in Artificial Gas Lift. 2017. P 18: 19

Thus, for a specific injection rate the production rate is maximum. The amount of injection rate and its corresponding production depends on well properties.

Khamehchi et al. (2014) and Ranjan et al. (2015) used an artificial neural network for predicting the optimum injection rate. They used the data of production flow and well test and created their model based on that. Their model's input were well parameters and the output was the optimum injection rate and its corresponding production rate. It is clear that for this type of optimization there is a model in reality, one which has been created using optimum points and can predict the optimum point of the new cases.

One of the limitations related to production is the water cut of each well. In fact, the water cut should not exceed a maximum. There are some other limitations related to injection and production. For example, in a gas allocation optimization problem, Tapabrata assumed a maximum limit for the injection rate of each well. Injection pressure depends on the used compressor and due to the difficulty of changing the compressor, in some problems it is considered as a constraint for the optimizer.

Some other limitations are such that production should be higher than a minimum (for example to escape liquid loading. In addition, the capacity of facilities in the gas lift system can be a constraint for the problem. This limitation causes the production reduction of other wells. [1]

Gas reservoirs are produced by expansion of the gas contained in the reservoir.

The high compressibility of the gas relative to the water in the reservoir (either connate water or underlying aquifer) make the gas expansion the dominant drive mechanism. Relative to oil reservoirs, the material balance calculation for gas reservoirs is rather simple. A major challenge in gas field development is to ensure a long sustainable plateau (typically 10 years) to attain a good sales price for the gas; the customer usually requires a reliable supply of gas at an agreed rate over many years. The RF for gas reservoirs depends on how low the abandonment pressure can be reduced, which is why compression facilities are often provided on surface. Typical RFs are in the range 50–80%.

3.2.1. Smart Methods

Using smart methods is an innovative way to increase the oil production. The smart fields can optimize the production in the long run. The first use of smart field methods dates back to the 1960s. There are currently much

[1] Ehsan Khamehchi • Mohammad Reza Mahdiani: Gas Allocation Optimization Methods in Artificial Gas Lift. 2017. P 27

more advanced technologies in this area that contain a design of completion methods and downhole instruments and sensors for pressure, temperature and fluid flow. These data are transformed to the surface for analysis and optimization. In addition, the smart technologies can be extended to surface facilities such as the compressor and surface valves. Smart field development can be regarded as a method for increasing the total production which consists of sensors, data accusation and reservoir optimization.

Camponogara et al. (2010) studied the smart field applicability in gas allocation optimization methods. Their method consisted of an algorithm that was allocating gas to some wells by considering the constraints. In this study, they assumed that all wells are equipped with pressure and temperature sensors and each well has its own controller for lift gas rate. The controller tries to assign the injection rates in order to maximize the oil production.

Another schematic of gas lift automation is shown in the Fig. As this figure shows, the system can be updated by information of the sensors (PT: pressure and temperature). Using this data from downhole and surface and analyzing them can be a method for watching the reservoir performance or some kind of well test. Based on the gained data, the system controls the flow (FC). [1]

([1])Ehsan Khamehchi • Mohammad Reza Mahdiani: Gas Allocation Optimization Methods in Artificial Gas Lift. 2017. P 32: 33

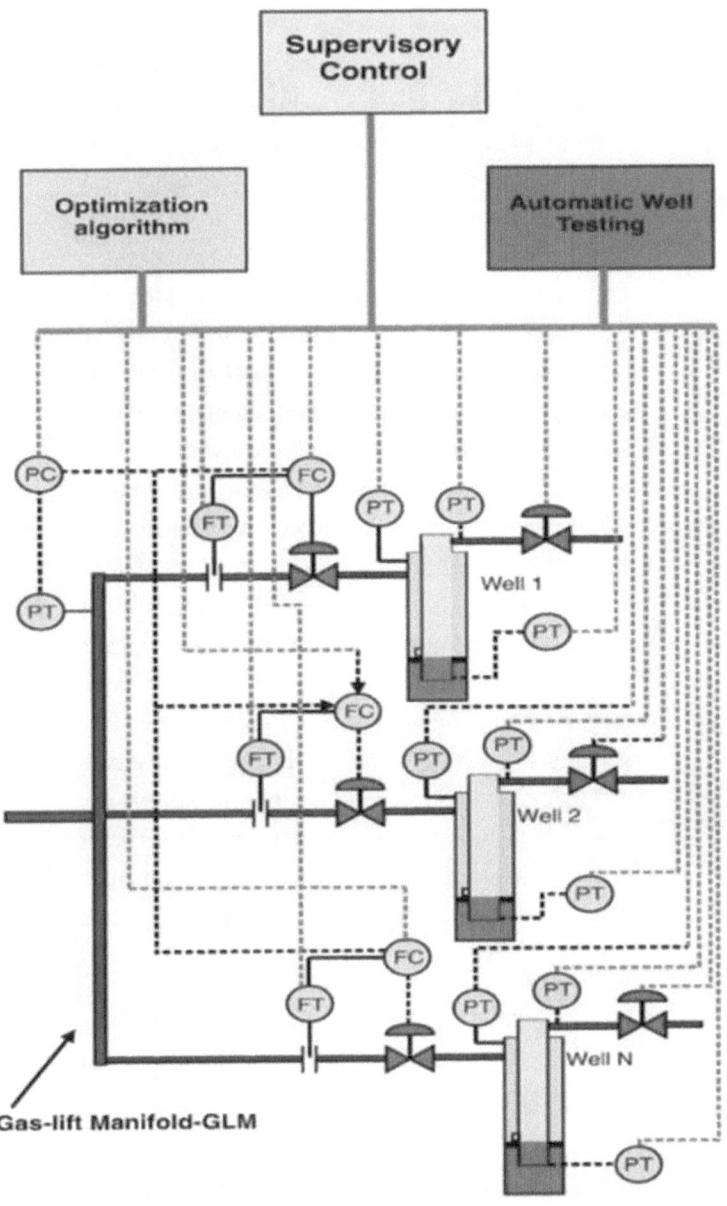

The rise in the amount of proven reserves of natural gas came from eliminating flaring in new oil wells, from finding new sources of the gas, in coal seams for example, and by discovering pockets of methane very deep in Earth's crust. This last type of natural gas exists at a very high temperature. Fortunately, methane is stable and does not decompose readily even at elevated temperatures. These methane pockets have no coal or oil near them and their origin is somewhat mysterious. A possible hypothesis for its origin is that this methane is the end product of the digestion of hydrocarbons by bacteria that exist deep in the Earth. However, Professor Thomas Gold of Cornell University has postulated that this methane is part of the primeval stuff of the universe. He believes there might be almost an infinite supply. Not many scientists believe this but if it is true, the reserves are incalculable. In any case lots of natural gas exists deep within Earth. This source is difficult and expensive to find but cheap to exploit once it is found. We do not know for sure how much is buried there. [1]

Another possible store of natural gas is methane hydrate. There are huge deposits of it widely distributed but deep underground.

---

[1]Sidney Borowitz: FAREWELL FOSSIL FUELS Reviewing America's. Energy Policy. Plenum Press, New York in 1999. P 74

Methane hydrate consists of single molecules of methane trapped within crystalline cages formed by frozen water molecules. It had been discovered in the early part of the 19th century but had not been studied by geologists because it was found under conditions of temperature and pressure which are difficult to explore. The discovery of sporadic pockets of methane hydrate a few decades ago led several researchers to estimate how much might be in the ground.

Beginning in the 1990s, much more data have been discovered. These new data seem to confirm an estimate made by geologist Gordon MacDonald, Director of the Institute for Applied Systems in Laxenberg, Austria in the 1980s, that methane hydrate deposits probably constitute the largest store of carbon that we know of underground. Others have conjectured these deposits might exceed all of the known reserves of coal, oil, and conventional natural gas. This conjecture has recently been given added weight by a discovery of lodes of methane hydrate hundreds of meters below the ocean bed off the coast of North Carolina. Researchers found methane hydrate and free methane there in concentrations about ten times previous estimates. [1]

---

[1] Sidney Borowitz: FAREWELL FOSSIL FUELS Reviewing America' s. Energy Policy. Plenum Press, New York in 1999. P 75

The dominant component in natural gases is methane (CH4). Others are mainly paraffinic hydrocarbons, such as ethane, propane, and butanes. Natural gas may also contain a small proportion of C5 hydrocarbons which is liquid fraction when separated at the surface.

Gas reservoirs may produce dry gas or wet gas depending on the content of light hydrocarbon (C5 hydrocarbons) in the natural gas. Gas reservoirs are thus classified into dry gas reservoir and wet gas reservoir. Their chief characters are described below. [1]

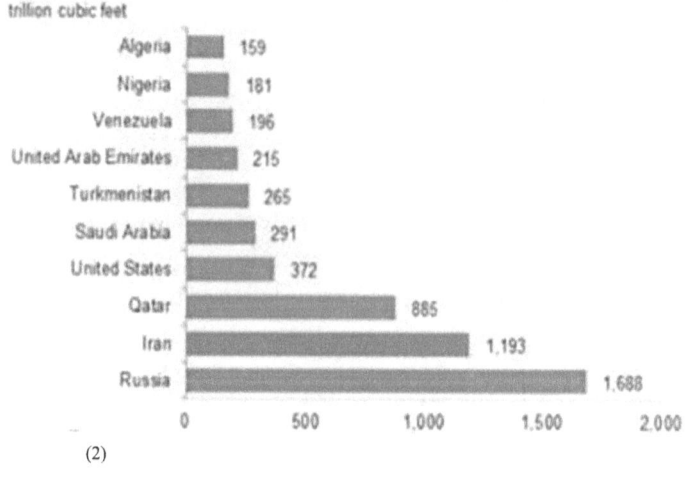

(2)

---

[1] Xuetao Hu • Shuyong Hu Fayang Jin • Su Huang: Physics of petroleum Reservoirs, Petroleum Industry Press, Beijing, China 2017. P 180
[2] Iakovos Alhadeff: USA Russia & China in the Middle East. Free ebook.net 2014. P 11

Table 1: International shale gas reserves
Source: EIA World Shale Resource Assessments

No.	Country	Trillion Cubic Feet (tcf)	Trillion Cubic Metre (tcm)
1	China	1115	31.6
2	Argentina	802	22.7
3	Algeria	707	20.0
4	US	623	17.6
5	Canada	573	16.2
6	Mexico	545	15.4
7	Australia	429	12.2
8	South Africa	390	11.0
9	Russia	285	8.1

10	Brazil	245	6.9
11	United Arab Emirates	205	5.8
12	Venezuela	167	4.7
	World	7577	214.5

(1)

From the perspective of natural gas supply, domestic natural gas production mainly concentrates in three oil and gas reservoirs including Talimu Oil and Gas Field, Southwest Oil and Gas Field and Changqing Oil and Gas field. Imported natural gas has become a effective supplement to China's natural gas supply. From the perspective of consumption, natural gas mostly is used in chemical industry and other industrial application, accounting for more than half of the total consumption. As the resident income increased lately, citizen's demand for natural gas is on a sharp rise. [2]

3.2.2. Dry Gas Reservoir

A dry gas reservoir is found initially with hydrocarbons in the gas phase alone, and

---

[1] World Energy Resources. World Energy Council. 2016. P 15: 16
[2] Jinjun Xue • Zhongxiu Zhao • Yande Dai • Bo Wang: Green Low-Carbon Development in China. Springer International Publishing Switzerland 2013. P 86

without liquid hydrocarbons accompanied in the reservoir. During the production of such reservoirs, no liquid hydrocarbons are separated from the gas whether at surface conditions or in the reservoir. Besides conventional gas reservoirs, dry gas reservoirs also include unconventional gas resources, such as coalbed methane (trapped in underground coal deposits), fractured shales containing gas, among Others. [1]

The initial condition for the dry gas is outside the two-phase envelope, and is to the right of the critical point, confirming that the fluid initially exists as a single-phase gas. As the reservoir is produced, the pressure drops under isothermal conditions, as indicated by the vertical line. Since the initial temperature is higher than the maximum temperature of the two-phase envelope (the cricondotherm – typically less

---

[1] Xuetao Hu • Shuyong Hu Fayang Jin • Su Huang: Physics of petroleum Reservoirs, Petroleum Industry Press, Beijing, China 2017. P 180

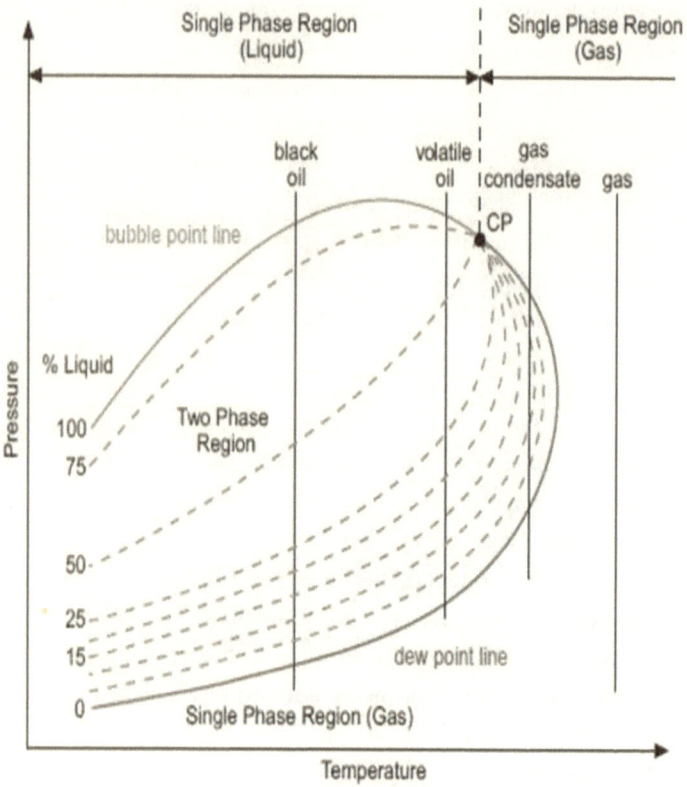

than 0C for a dry gas), the reservoir conditions of temperature and pressure never fall inside the two-phase region, indicating that the composition and phase of the fluid in the reservoir remains constant.

In addition, the separator temperature and pressure of the surface facilities are typically outside the two-phase envelope, so no liquids form during separation. This makes the prediction of the produced fluids during development very simple, and gas sales contracts can be agreed with the confidence that the fluid composition will remain constant during field life in the case of a dry gas. [1]

3.2.3. Wet Gas Reservoir

A wet reservoir contains all hydrocarbons in the gas phase, as in a dry gas reservoir. During the process of pressure decline upon production, the gas remaining in the reservoir would be entirely in a single phase, without any condensation in the subsurface reservoir. However, a small portion of the gas produced through the wells condenses to liquids owing to the decline in pressure and temperature at surface conditions. So, a wet gas reservoir will produce small amounts of liquid oil. This phenomenon is due to the presence of some heavier hydrocarbons in the reservoir gas that condense under surface conditions. [2]

the Middle East and northern Africa have very large conventional natural gas reserves and are significant providers of LNG, mostly to the Asian markets. Four Middle Eastern countries, Iran (16 %), Qatar (14 %),

---

[1]Frank Jahn, Mark Cook and Mark Graham: HYDROCARBON EXPLORATION AND PRODUCTION. 2ND EDITION. Elsevier B.V. 2008. P 119: 120
[2]Xuetao Hu • Shuyong Hu Fayang Jin • Su Huang: Physics of petroleum Reservoirs, Petroleum Industry Press, Beijing, China 2017. P 180

Saudi Arabia (4 %) and the UAE (3 %) have over a third of global deposits and Qatar is the world's largest supplier of LNG. However, the "Export Land Model" is also applicable to natural gas exports, with production increases in Iran, Saudi Arabia, and the UAE being used predominantly to serve the domestic market. The balance between increased local demand and production levels will dictate the ability of the region to increase exports. [1]

Central Asia has become a highly promising source of natural gas exports. Substantial reserves have been discovered, facilitating production which is far in excess of local demand. A gas pipeline to China has been completed and a connection to Europe is scheduled to be completed in 2017. Gas exports from the region will double during the next decade with China taking about half of all exports. Such exports will become more critical as Indonesia and Malaysia switch from being net exporters to net importers in the next few years. Increases in Australian exports will also help fill the gap left by Indonesia and Malaysia. The rapidly growing economies of India and China, together with a Japan without its nuclear power, will require increasing levels of LNG supplies. China and Australia also have significant shale

---

[1] Roger Boyd: Energy and the Financial System Springer Cham Heidelberg New York Dordrecht London 2013. P 34: 35

gas resources that have yet to be developed. With an authoritarian government that could possibly force through shale gas development in the former and low population densities in the latter, both countries may be successful in exploiting these resources. [1]

Russia owns 32.6 trillion cubic meters (Tcm) of gas reserves, an amount equal to 25 percent of the world's total proven reserves. Around 70 percent of these reserves are located in onshore Western Siberia and 10 percent in onshore European regions. Some 11 percent are located off shore on the Russian continental shelf, mainly in the Barents Sea. Around 40 percent of the Russian gas reserves are concentrated in hard-to-reach areas, thus making both exploration and production from the fields more technologically difficult and expensive.

Russia exported 119 Bcm of gas to Europe in 2014, mainly through the four pipelines that constitute the basic structure of the Russian gas export industry: The Brotherhood Pipeline, the Northern Lights Pipeline, the Yamal-Europe Pipeline and the Nord Stream Pipeline.

In the aftermath of the 2014 Ukraine crisis, Russia remained committed to export its gas to Europe, confirming that the EU-Russia

---

[1] Roger Boyd: Energy and the Financial System Springer Cham Heidelberg New York Dordrecht London 2013. P 35

gas partnership should be read as a situation of mutual interdependence rather than unilateral dependence of Europe. In other words, Russia is willing to sell and to continue to sell gas to Europe, as it represents the cornerstone of its export architecture. Russia considers a fundamental prerequisite to ensure the stability of this trade relation, to reduce the role of Ukraine as a transit corridor for Russian gas to Europe, in order to avoid transit problems as occurred in 2006 and 2009. However, the target announced in 2015 to reduce the transit through Ukraine to zero can also be seen as politically motivated. [1]

In terms of gas reserve estimations, the recent years have been very volatile for Algeria. In fact, the Energy Information Administration (EIA) estimated in 2013, the country's technically recoverable shale gas resources at about 20 Tcm, the third largest in the world after China and Argentina.

These positive developments on the unconventional side have been accompanied by surprisingly negative news on the conventional side, with the country downgrading its estimated conventional gas reserves from 4.5 Tcm to 2.7 Tcm at the end of 2015.

---

[1] Simone Tagliapietra: Energy Relations in the Euro-Mediterranean. 2017. P 49

But the assessment of gas reserves has not been the only volatile element in the country's gas sector. Also, production, consumption and export trends have consistently changed over the last years. [1]

The US Energy Information Administration said average first-of-the-month prices used to calculate US reserves dropped in 2016 compared with 2015. Natural gas and crude oil decreased by a respective 6% and 15% during the period.

EIA's report, US Crude Oil and Natural Gas Proved Reserves, Yearend 2016, showed a 5% increase in proved gas reserves to 341.1 tcf. Oil and condensate increased by 3% in the Lower 48 states, but reserves in Alaska and the federal offshore decreased bringing the yearend 2016 reserves to 35.2 billion bbl, which was a net decline of 17 million bbl.

EIA highlighted onshore proved crude and condensate reserves that increased by 846 million bbl (3%) in the Lower 48, but these were offset by the 865 million bbl decline in reserves for Alaska, and federal and state offshore areas. The administration noted that higher development costs in these areas most likely prohibited reserves growth in most recent low-price environment.

[1] Simone Tagliapietra: Energy Relations in the Euro-Mediterranean. 2017. P 57

Texas and Oklahoma showed the highest net increases in 2016, with the liquids-rich shale plays in the Permian basin—Wolfcamp and Bone Springs—and the SCOOP and STACK plays in Oklahoma's Anadarko basin (OGJ Online, Jan. 30, 2018).

Despite these gains, EIA said crude and condensate production slipped by 6% from 2015. Total reserves were kept constant from new field additions and new reservoirs identified in previously discovered fields. Existing field extensions also kept US reserves buoyed against production offsets.

Pennsylvania showed the largest net natural gas increase, adding 6.1 tcf to US proved reserves. The increase is attributed to ongoing Marcellus shale development in the Appalachian basin. Oklahoma struck again in the top performers during the period as the state added 3.7 tcf of natural gas reserves from the SCOOP and STACK plays (OGJ Online, Feb. 18, 2018). Ohio's 3.1 tcf addition is attributed to recent developments in the Utica shale play (OGJ Online, Jan. 9, 2018).

US natural gas production showed a minor 1% decrease from 2015, according to EIA. Shale gas once again dominated US reserves growth, increasing to 62% of reserves in 2016 from the 2015 share of 54%. Natural gas reserves additions exceeded production by more than 30% in 2016.

EIA reported that net revisions in US 2016 oil and gas reserves were below its 2015 report, while extensions and discoveries remained at the same level. [1]

Compared to a dry gas, a wet gas contains a larger fraction of the C2–C6 components, and hence its phase envelope is moved down and to the right. Whilst the reservoir conditions remain outside the two-phase envelope, so that the reservoir fluid composition remains constant and the gaseous phase is maintained, the separator conditions are inside the two-phase envelope. As the dew point is crossed, the heavier components condense as liquids in the separator. The exact volume percent of liquids which condense depends upon the separator conditions and the spacing of the iso-vol lines for the mixture (the lines of constant liquid percentage shown in Figure 6.20). These heavier components are valuable as light ends of the fractionation range of petroleum and sell at a premium price. It is usually worthwhile to recover these liquids, and to leave the sales gas as a dry gas (predominantly methane, CH_4). Note that the term wet gas does not refer to water content, but

---

[1]Tayvis Dunnahoe: OGJ Exploration. 2018

rather to the gas composition containing more of the heavier hydrocarbons than a dry gas. [1]

3.2.4. Gas condensate

The initial temperature of a gas condensate lies between the critical temperature and the cricondotherm. The fluid therefore exists at initial conditions in the reservoir as a gas, but on pressure depletion the dew point line is reached, at which point liquids condense in the reservoir. As can be seen from the Figure, the volume percent of liquids is low, typically insufficient for the saturation of the liquid in the pore space to reach the critical saturation beyond which the liquid phase becomes mobile.

These liquids therefore remain trapped in the reservoir as an immobile phase. Since these liquids are valuable products, there is an incentive to avoid this condensation in the reservoir by maintaining the reservoir pressure above the dew point. This is the reason for considering recycling of gas in these types of reservoir.

Gas is produced to surface separators which are used to extract the heavier ends of the mixture (typically the C_{5+} components). The dry gas is then compressed and re-injected into the

---

[1]Frank Jahn, Mark Cook and Mark Graham: HYDROCARBON EXPLORATION AND PRODUCTION. 2ND EDITION. Elsevier B.V. 2008. P 120: 121

reservoir to maintain the pressure above the dew point. As the recycling progresses, the reservoir composition becomes leaner (less heavy components), until eventually it is not economic to separate and compress the dry

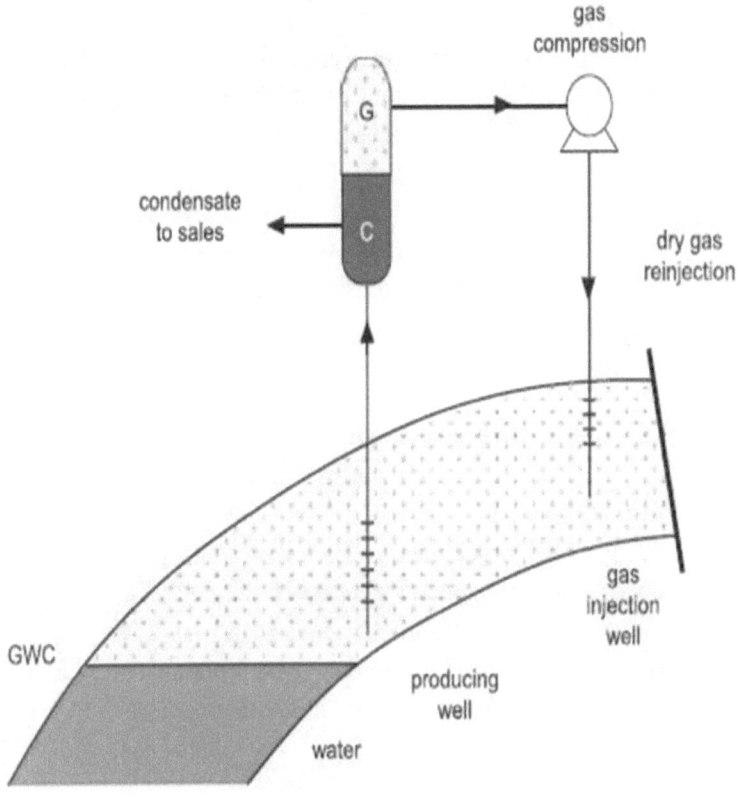

gas, at which point the reservoir pressure is 'blown down' as for a wet gas reservoir.

The sales profile for a recycling scheme consists of early sales of condensate liquids and delayed sale of gas. An alternative method of keeping the reservoir above the dew point but avoiding the deferred gas sales is by water injection, but this is rarely done as gas trapped behind an advancing gas–water contact represents a significant loss.

The Figure shows that as the pressure is reduced below the dew point, the volume of liquid in the two-phase mixture initially increases. This contradicts the common observation of the fraction of liquids in a volatile mixture reducing as the pressure is dropped (vaporization) and explains why the fluids are sometimes referred to as retrograde gas condensates. [1]

3.2.5. Tight Gas Reservoirs

Matrix permeability in tight sand formations may be very low due to the depositional processes, or because of the post-depositional diagenetic events. If the tight gas reservoir is naturally fractured, then the gas flow is mainly controlled by the open undamaged natural fractures that are connected to the wellbore.

The rock matrix may primarily be composed of micro-pores where average pore

---

[1]Frank Jahn, Mark Cook and Mark Graham: HYDROCARBON EXPLORATION AND PRODUCTION. 2ND EDITION. Elsevier B.V. 2008. P 121: 122

throat aperture is very small, causing tremendous amounts of potential capillary pressure energy suction. In tight formations that are water-wet in nature, the capillary forces cause liquid to be imbibed and held in the capillary pores. This causes the critical water saturation and irreducible water saturation to be high in the tight formations. Initial water saturation in tight gas reservoirs might vary depending on the timing of gas migration. A tight gas reservoir may have normal initial water saturation or in some cases sub-normal due to water phase vaporization into the gas phase as shown in Fig. A sub-normal provides relatively a higher effective permeability for gas phase, close to absolute permeability. The initial water saturation might also be more than critical water saturation if the hydrocarbon trap is created during or after the gas migration time. In the case of high initial water saturation, relative permeability to gas may be very low.

The reservoir geometry of tight gas reservoirs depends on their deposition environment: they normally consist of numerous reservoir layers/lenses, which are discontinuous both vertically and laterally in a thick complex sedimentary system, and separated by non-reservoir shales. The stacks of isolated lenses of sand bodies may vary in characteristics, shape and volume as shown in Fig. The recoverable gas in place in tight gas reservoirs is mainly controlled by the sand lens width, and the effect of sand lens length is not very significant. Horizontal deviated well drilling can help intersecting as many of the sand lenses as possible, and effectively increase lateral reservoir exposure to wellbore.

Tight gas reservoirs productivity may also be affected by in situ stresses as they can control hydraulic fractures propagation, reservoir flow regimes, permeability anisotropy, wellbore instability and long-term production performance. Tight gas sandstones are typically very stiff rocks capable of supporting high, or even extreme deviatoric stresses.

Tight sand formations commonly have wellbore instability issues during drilling, which causes large wellbore breakouts and washouts across the tight sand intervals. The wellbore instability issues in tight formations can be reduced by drilling the well in the minimum stress direction.

In tight sand reservoirs, understanding of the relative magnitude of in situ stresses and their direction, and their relationship with permeability are essential for tight gas development. Tight gas reservoirs are normally heterogeneous and anisotropic in nature, where permeability is a direction dependent property. The permeability anisotropy may be further enhanced by the pattern of earlier geological deformation and be amplified by in situ stresses.

In cased-hole perforated wells completed in tight sand, well productivity may significantly be controlled by perforation parameters. Perforation performance depends on factors such as length of down-hole penetration, shot phasing, and shot density. Deep penetration, at least 50 % beyond the damage thickness, is needed to effectively connect wellbore to undamaged rock. Perforation efficiency in tight gas reservoirs is affected by the high rock strength that makes penetration of perforation jet to be significantly reduced compared with equivalent sandstone of higher porosity. Using deep penetrating perforation charges run with shock absorbers can mitigate damage to perforation tunnels and reduce the skin fact. [1]

3.2.6. Unconventional Gas

The hydrocarbon sources from conventional reservoirs are decreasing rapidly. Because global energy consumption is increasing steadily at the same time, conventional reserves alone cannot meet the growing demand. According to EIA Annual Energy Outlook 2015 (EIA 2015a, b), total primary energy consumption will grow by 8.6

---

[1] Nick Bahrami: Evaluating Factors Controlling Damage and Productivity in Tight Gas Reservoirs. Doctoral Thesis. Springer International Publishing Switzerland 2013. P 1: 3

quadrillion Btu (8.9 %) from 97.1 quadrillion Btu in 2013 to 105.7 quadrillion Btu in 2040. There is a pressing need for alternative sources of hydrocarbon energy resources. From technical and economic points of view, the expensive sustainable and renewable energy sources cannot compete with the relatively cheap nonrenewable fossil fuels. Therefore, the immediate alternatives for conventional hydrocarbon would be found in unconventional oil and gas resources.

As shown in Fig. a, these unconventional resources come in many forms and include tight gas, shale gas, coal bed methane (CBM), tight oil, shale oil, and oil shale. Figure b shows worldwide gas resource pyramids that include the general characteristics and global endowment for each resource. Endowment is the summation of cumulative gas production, reserves, and undiscovered gas. Figure b shows that the total natural gas endowment, excluding gas hydrates, is approximately 68,000 trillion cubic feet (Tcf) and about 70 % of it is estimated in tight and shale gas.

Decades ago, geologists knew there were vast natural gas resources locked in shale rock deep beneath the earth's surface over much of North America. However, it has been remained as a hard-to-produce resource for a long time. As exploration and production companies use special drilling and formation stimulation (e.g., hydraulic fracturing) techniques to make shale reservoir production economically viable, shale gas has been the focus of gas exploration and production in the United

(a)
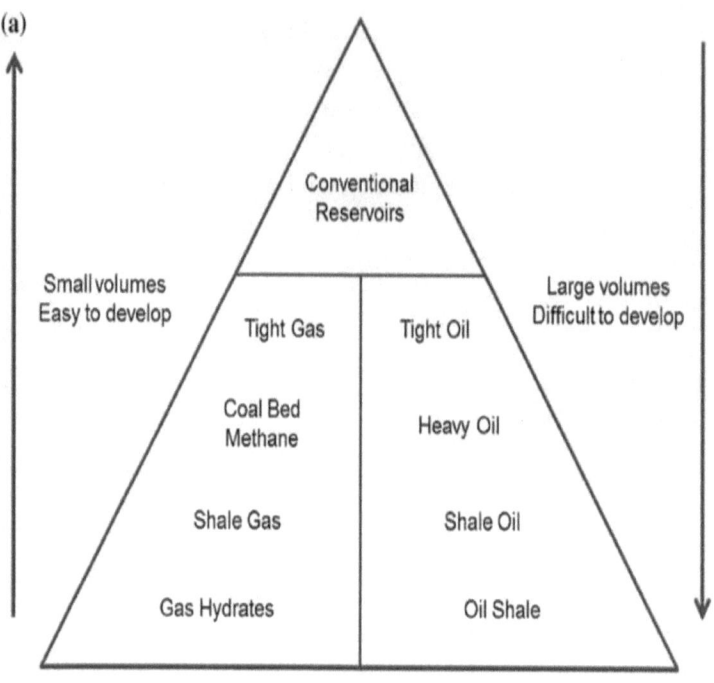

(b)
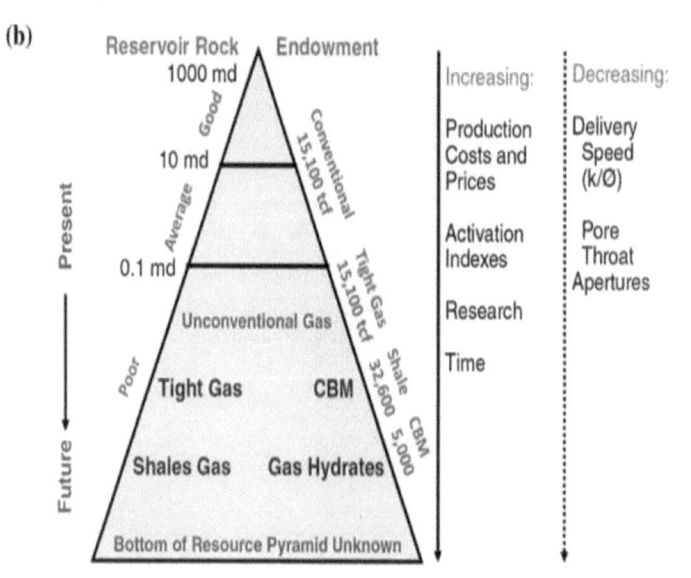

States and in other countries. Based on a recent EIA report (EIA 2013a), there is an estimated 7299 Tcf of technically recoverable shale gas resource to be found in some 95 basins in 41 countries.

As source rocks for most oil and gas deposits, technically recoverable (although not necessarily economically recoverable) gas shale is abundant across the globe. It is also located in a very wide range of geographical regions, and in many of the nations with the highest energy consumption. For certain nations, shale gas, therefore, has the potential to reduce energy prices and dependence on other nations, hence impact on both the political and economic outlook. However, the prospects for and significance of shale gas are greater where there is lack of existing conventional gas production, where there is a lack of existing conventional gas production, where there is proximity to demand (i.e., population), and where some form of existing gas distribution infrastructure exists.

Shale gas resources have received great attention because of their potential to supply the world with an immense amount of energy and the depletion of conventional reservoirs. Shale gas reservoirs have some features dissimilar to those of conventional reservoirs. Typically, shale gas reservoirs include conductive natural fractures that substantially influence well performance.

Because shale gas reservoirs have narrow thickness and infinite lateral extension, horizontal wells are usually applied to increase production by augmenting the contact area of the wellbore and the pay zone. Shale matrix has extremely low permeability. To exploit ultra-low permeability reservoirs, hydraulic fracturing technology has been proved to be an effective means. Hydraulic fracturing induces fractures with enormously high permeability and makes fracture networks around the wellbore. Shale gas is stored in both free gas and adsorbed gas. Therefore, shale gas reservoirs show a long period of changing behavior and intricate flow regimes, which makes understanding the pressure behavior of shale gas reservoirs important.

Following notable successes in shale gas production in the USA, to the point where that country now produces more shale gas than gas from the conventional sources, other countries are pursuing the same course. Even so, in order to be successful in the exploration and the development of shale gas plays, a vast knowledge of the shales is required. The aim of this book is to provide some guidance on the major factors involved in evaluation shale gas reservoirs. [1]

---

[1]Kun Sang Lee • Tae Hong Kim: Integrative Understanding of Shale Gas Reservoirs. 2016. P 1: 3

4. Separation of Natural Gas from Crude Oil

In reservoirs, crude oil usually contains a great deal of dissolved gas due to high pressure. When produced out from the hot, high-pressure reservoir to the surface, crude oil experiences the reduction in pressure and temperature. During the process of pressure deplete, the dissolved gas in oil tends to escape from the oil. At surface conditions, a great deal of gas evolves from the oil. For the convenience of transportation, the dissolved gas must be completely separated from the oil at surface conditions. The physical separation or oil–gas separation of the crude oil from wells is one of the basic operations in crude oil production.

Essentially, oil–gas separation is a phenomenon of gas evolving from crude oil because of pressure deplete. It may occur in reservoirs, within wellbores, and in surface production. The separation of oil and gas in surface production are primarily concerned here. In surface production, based on the way of pressure deplete, two methods for gas–oil separation are developed: flash separation and stage separation. [1]

---

[1]Xuetao Hu • Shuyong Hu Fayang Jin • Su Huang: Physics of petroleum Reservoirs, Petroleum Industry Press, Beijing, China 2017. P 249

5. Estimated Volumes of Remaining Oil and Gas Resources

Proved reserves are the volume of known oil and gas accumulations that can be produced at a profit under existing economic and operating conditions. Estimates of world-proved reserves of oil and gas are compiled using best available information by several organizations including the International Energy Agency, IHS Energy, and BP. Proved reserves of oil and gas are not routinely reported in many countries.

In fact, some of the largest producers consider reserves as state secrets. This lack of transparent reporting has led some to question the size of global reserves giving credence to predictions of imminent production declines. However, though differing in detail the reserves estimated by different agencies are similar in estimated overall size. As of the end of 2009, BP estimated globally proved reserves of 1,333 billion barrels of oil (BBO), equivalent to over 45 years of production at 2009 rates. With the exception of 237 billion barrels of oil in the Canadian oil sands, these reserves are entirely of conventional oil. BP also estimated globally proved reserves of natural gas at 6,621 trillion cubic feet (TCF), equivalent to 63 years of production. These reserves are predominantly conventional gas.

In addition to prove reserves, there are undiscovered resources and "contingent resources" that are currently noncommercial but could probably be produced under different economic conditions. The most recent comprehensive global estimate of undiscovered oil and gas resources was published by the USGS in 2000.

This was a geologically based study of 128 geologic provinces that included the producing basins that accounted for more than 95% of the world's known oil and gas outside of the United States. The study also examined the discovery history of each province up to 1996. The report included probabilistic estimates of the volumes of conventional oil, gas, and natural gas liquids that might be added to prove reserves from new field discoveries in the studied provinces from the 1996 baseline. The assessment estimated that there was a 95% chance of discovering another 334 BBO of conventional oil and a 5% chance of discovering 1,107 BBO.

The median estimate, the 50% chance, was that 607 BBO of oil might yet be found in the studied provinces. For conventional natural gas, the assessment estimated that there was a 95% chance of discovering another 2,299 TCF and a 5% chance of discovering 8,174 TCF. The median estimate was that 4,333 of natural gas might be found in the studied provinces.

More recent estimates by the USGS that have concentrated on specific regions of the world suggest that on balance their 2000 estimates are probably reasonable estimates of the global picture though there is need for revision in some areas.

A 2010 study estimates 17% less undiscovered oil and 20% less undiscovered natural gas than in the 2000 assessment in eight basins in Southeast Asia; however, there had been at least 10 years of discoveries between the two assessments.

Furthermore, the 2010 assessment examined a number of additional basins in Southeast Asia resulting in an overall increase in estimated undiscovered oil of 71% and natural gas by 66%. The 2008 USGS assessment of the Arctic revised down the estimate of undiscovered oil by 48%, largely because of a reappraisal of the West Siberian Basin, but increased the estimate of natural gas by 21% by including a number of basins not in the 2000 assessment.

The USGS 2000 assessment also estimated the amount of reserve growth that could be anticipated to 2025 for fields that had been discovered prior to 1996.

The median estimate for reserve growth for conventional oil was 612 BBO and for conventional natural gas 3,305 trillion cubic feet. At the time of writing, the midpoint of the time interval has been reached over which reserve growth was predicted and a substantial amount of the predicted reserve growth has already occurred. It seems unreasonable, however, to assume that reserve growth will cease in 2025 and interestingly King, using a different methodology and separate data from that used by the USGS, estimated future reserve growth of oil at between 200 to 1,000 BBO – almost exactly the same range that the USGS predicted would occur from 1996.

provides an estimate of remaining oil resources at the end of 2007. The proved reserve numbers are from BP and are slightly lower than those of EIA. The estimated volume of oil in undiscovered fields is revised down from the median estimate in the USGS 2000 assessment because 16.5% of that volume had been discovered by 2007. However, it should be noted that this may be conservative as the 2000 assessment did not include the United States and many geologic basins that have relatively small volumes of discovered oil or where there has been little or no exploration. The reserve growth numbers are based on King for crude oil, as discussed above, and 50% of the USGS 2000 estimated median reserve growth for NGL that was predicted to occur between 1996 and 2025. The oil sand reserve and resource estimates are for Canada and Venezuela only though there are smaller oil sand accumulations in several other countries. The shale oil estimate is from Dyni. The estimated remaining conventional oil is equivalent to 79 years of annual production at 2009 rates. The estimated unconventional oil adds up to the equivalent of 125 years of annual production.

Global reserves of natural gas in 2010 were estimated at a little over 6,600 TCF by BP and EIA. Taking into account discoveries since 1996 and revising down the median estimate of gas in undiscovered fields from the USGS 2000 assessment, and also assuming 50% of the estimated reserve growth has taken place, the remaining conventional natural gas resources are estimated at approximately 11,850 TCF, equivalent to about 87 years of annual production at 2009 rates.

Estimating global abundance of unconventional gas resources is difficult because development of these resources is largely in its infancy, especially outside of North America. Recently published estimates of recoverable shale gas resources in the United States and Canada vary between 50 and 1,000 TCF. Estimates for the rest of the world would likely have an even larger range. It is particularly important to discriminate between "in-place resources" and those that are economically recoverable. The USGS estimated that the

United States has 700 TCF of CBM gas in place but only 100 TCF that would be economically recoverable.

As 20.5 TCF was produced over the following 13 years under a major drilling effort, 100 TCF may be an optimistic estimate of ultimate recovery. The USGS also suggested that global in-place CBM gas resources may be as high as 7,500 TCF but recoverable resources may well be an order of magnitude lower. Australia, for example, has 9% of the world's coal resources and an estimated 153 TCF of recoverable CBM gas, of which 90% is currently sub-economic or not yet proven by drilling. While extraordinarily large estimates of unconventional gas resources (particularly for hydrates) should be regarded with some skepticism from an economic perspective, there is ample evidence that unconventional gas resources are abundant. In the United States, which has a wide variety of geologic basins, 50% of the gas produced in 2010 was unconventional and it is not unreasonable to suppose that globally the abundance of unconventional gas resources is of a similar scale to conventional gas resources. [1]

---

[1]Ripudaman Malhotra: Fossil Energy. Springer Science+Business Media New York 2013. P 18: 20

6. Oil recovery
6.1. Principles of Enhanced Oil Recovery

Traditionally, oil recovery operations have been subdivided into three stages: primary, secondary, and tertiary. Historically, these stages describe the production from a reservoir in a chronological sense. Primary production, the initial production stage, results from the displacement energy naturally existing in reservoirs. Secondary recovery, the second stage of operations, usually is implemented after primary production exhausted. Traditional secondary recovery processes include waterflooding, pressure maintenance, and gas injection. Tertiary recovery, the third stage of production, is that obtained after waterflooding. Tertiary processes used miscible gases, chemicals, and/or thermal energy to displace additional oil after the secondary recovery process became uneconomical. [1]

In other situations, the so-called tertiary process might be applied as a secondary operation in lieu of waterflooding. This action might be dictated by such factors as the nature of the tertiary process, availability of injectants, and economics. For example, if a waterflood before application of the tertiary process diminishes the overall effectiveness, then the

---

[1] Xuetao Hu • Shuyong Hu Fayang Jin • Su Huang: Physics of petroleum Reservoirs, Petroleum Industry Press, Beijing, China 2017. P 466

waterflooding stage might reasonably be bypassed. [1]

  Primary recovery refers to the use of natural energy presenting in reservoirs as the main source of energy for the displacement of oil to producing wells. These natural energy sources are solution–gas drive, gas cap drive, natural water drive, fluid and rock expansion, and gravity drainage. The particular mechanism of lifting oil to the surface, once it is in the wellbore, is not a factor in the classification scheme.

  Secondary recovery results from the augmentation of natural energy through injection of water or gas to displace oil toward producing wells. Gas injection, in this case, is either into a gas cap for pressure maintenance and gas cap expansion or into oil-column wells to displace oil immiscibly according to relative permeability and volumetric sweepout considerations. Gas processes based on other mechanisms, such as oil swelling, oil viscosity reduction, or favorable phase behavior, are considered EOR processes. An immiscible gas displacement is not as efficient as a waterflood and is used infrequently as a secondary recovery process today. Today,

---

[1]Xuetao Hu • Shuyong Hu Fayang Jin • Su Huang: Physics of petroleum Reservoirs, Petroleum Industry Press, Beijing, China 2017. P 466

waterflooding is almost synonymous with the secondary recovery classification. [1]

Enhanced oil recovery (tertiary oil recovery) is the incremental ultimate oil that can be recovered from a petroleum reservoir over oil that can be obtained by primary and secondary recovery methods. Enhanced oil recovery methods offer prospects for ultimately producing 30–60%, or more, of the reservoir's original oil-in-place.

Enhanced oil recovery processes use thermal, chemical, or fluid phase behavior effects to reduce or eliminate the capillary forces that trap oil within pores, to thin the oil or otherwise improve its mobility or to alter the mobility of the displacing fluids. In some cases, the effects of gravity forces, which ordinarily cause vertical segregation of fluids of different densities, can be minimized or even used to advantage. The various processes differ considerably in complexity, the physical mechanisms responsible for oil recovery, and the amount of experience that has been derived from field application. The degree to which the enhanced oil recovery methods are applicable in the future will depend on development of improved process technology. It will also

---

[1] Xuetao Hu • Shuyong Hu Fayang Jin • Su Huang: Physics of petroleum Reservoirs, Petroleum Industry Press, Beijing, China 2017. P 466

depend on improved understanding of fluid chemistry, phase behavior, and physical properties, and also on the accuracy of geology and reservoir engineering in characterizing the physical nature of individual reservoirs.

For taxation purposes, the Internal Revenue Service of the United States has listed the projects that qualify as enhanced oil recovery projects and are therefore available for a tax credit and these projects are:

1. Thermal recovery methods:

Thermal methods of recovery reduce the viscosity of the crude oil by heat so that it flows more easily into the production well.

(a) Steam drive injection – the continuous injection of steam into one set of wells (injection wells) or other injection source to effect oil displacement toward and production from a second set of wells (production wells).

(b) Cyclic steam injection – the alternating injection of steam and production of oil with condensed steam from the same well or wells.

(c) In situ combustion – the combustion of oil or fuel in the reservoir sustained by injection of air, oxygen-enriched air, oxygen, or supplemental fuel supplied from the surface to displace unburned oil toward producing wells.

This process may include the concurrent, alternating, or subsequent injection of water. Steam-based methods are the most advanced of all enhanced oil recovery methods in terms of field experience and thus have the least uncertainty in estimating performance, provided that a good reservoir description is available.

Steam processes are most often applied in reservoirs containing heavy crude oil, usually in place of rather than following secondary or primary methods. Commercial application of steam processes has been underway since the early 1960s.

2. Gas flood recovery methods:

(a) Miscible fluid displacement – the injection of gas (e.g., natural gas, enriched natural gas, a liquefied petroleum slug driven by natural gas, carbon dioxide, nitrogen, or flue gas) or alcohol into the reservoir at pressure levels such that the gas or alcohol and reservoir oil are miscible.

(b) Carbon dioxide–augmented waterflooding – the injection of carbonated water, or water and carbon dioxide, to increase waterflood efficiency.

(c) Immiscible carbon dioxide displacement – the injection of carbon dioxide into an oil reservoir to effect oil displacement under conditions in which miscibility with reservoir oil is not obtained; this process may include the concurrent, alternating, or subsequent injection of water.

(d) Immiscible nonhydrocarbon gas isplacement – the injection of nonhydrocarbon gas (e.g., nitrogen) into an oil reservoir, under conditions in which miscibility with reservoir oil is not obtained, to obtain a chemical or physical reaction (other than pressure) between the oil and the injected gas or between the oil and other reservoir fluids; this process may include the concurrent, alternating, or subsequent injection of water.

3. Chemical flood recovery methods:

Three enhanced oil recovery processes involve the use of chemicals – surfactant/polymer, polymer, and alkaline flooding. However, each reservoir has unique fluid and rock properties, and specific chemical systems must be designed for each individual application. The chemicals used, their concentrations in the slugs, and the slug sizes depend upon the specific properties of the fluids and the rocks involved and upon economic considerations.

(a) Surfactant flooding is a multiple-slug process involving the addition of surface-active chemicals to water. These chemicals reduce the capillary forces that trap the oil in the pores of the rock. The surfactant slug displaces the majority of the oil from the reservoir volume contacted, forming a flowing oil–water bank that is propagated ahead of the surfactant slug.

The principal factors that influence the surfactant slug design are interfacial properties, slug mobility in relation to the mobility of the oil–water bank, the persistence of acceptable slug properties and slug integrity in the reservoir, and cost.

(b) Microemulsion flooding also known as surfactant-polymer flooding involves injection of a surfactant system (e.g., a surfactant, hydrocarbon, cosurfactant, electrolyte, and water) to enhance the displacement of oil toward producing wells; and caustic flooding – the injection of water that has been made chemically basic by the addition of alkali metal hydroxides, silicates, or other chemicals.

(c) Polymer-augmented waterflooding – the injection of polymeric additives with water to improve the areal and vertical sweep efficiency of the reservoir by increasing the viscosity and decreasing the mobility of the water injected; polymer-augmented waterflooding does not include the injection of polymers for the purpose of modifying the injection profile of the wellbore or the relative permeability of various layers of the reservoir, rather than modifying the water-oil mobility ratio. [1]

Being a developed technology, EOR is implemented in carbon dioxide injection into geological formations. On commercial or research levels, in the year 2000, 84 projects were operational, worldwide, of which USA accounts for 72 projects, mostly located in the Permian Basin. Together, these projects produced 200,772 barrels (bbl) of oil per day, a small but meaningful fraction (0.3 %) of the 67.2 million bbl per day total of world-wide oil production that year. ONGC has formulated a plan for usage of CO_2 that is stripped from offshore sour gas at its Hazira facility for EOR at its onshore Ankleswar oil field, 70 km away. Roughly 1200 tonnes of CO_2 will be captured and transported to the oil field on a daily basis (440,000 tonnes of CO_2/year).

In majority of CO_2-EOR projects, a lot of CO_2 injected into the oil reservoir is temporarily stored because the withdrawing of an EOR project usually demands for the "blowing down"of the reservoir pressure to tap oil recovery, thus resulting in the release of CO_2, with a small but substantial amount of the injected CO_2 staying dissolved in the immobile oil. [1]

---

[1] Ripudaman Malhotra: Fossil Energy. Springer Science+Business Media New York 2013. P 38: 40

[1] V. Vishal • T.N. Singh: Geologic Carbon Sequestration. Springer International Publishing Switzerland 2016. P 13

There are four potential targets for the EOR-storage projects implementation

(1) Mature oilfields that experienced long periods of primary and secondary recovery, especially waterflooding

(2) Depleted oilfields that experienced the primary recovery phase and some secondary recovery method such as the artificial lift

(3) Depleted gas fields, and (4) Capillary transition zones (CTZ) and residual oil zones (ROZ) below the main pay zone (MPZ).

The target zone for the first three categories is the main pay zone (MPZ) which is above the water-oil contact or the water-gas contact. The initial water saturation in MPZ is at the residual water saturation. The MPZ is conventionally perforated for the primary and secondary recovery phases to avoid the excessive water production.

The CTZ is developed as the result of vertical equilibrium of the capillary forces and gravity forces under the static conditions between the water-oil and oil-gas zones. Residual oil zone (ROZ) is an attractive target for the EOR-storage operation.

The ROZ should not be confused with the capillary transition zone (CTZ). The residual oil zone may develop by the natural waterflood of the oil trap through a geologic time scale. The nature's waterflood process may be triggered after second stage tectonic activities such as basin tilt, breached seals, and uplift and lateral sweep an active aquifer exists.

There are three types of screening criteria for the identification of EOR-storage candidates: logistic, geological/reservoir, and crude oil criteria. There are few potential targets, if any, around the world that meet all these criteria.

The logistic screening criteria are often prioritized to the geological/reservoir or the crude oil criteria because the logistics determine the capital investments on the CO_2 capture and transport. [1]

6.1.1. ESTIMATION OF INITIAL OIL IN PLACE BY THE MATERIAL BALANCE METHOD FOR A SOLUTION GAS DRIVE RESERVOIR

The initial oil in place for a solution gas/depletion drive reservoir is estimated, utilizing the generalized material balance equation and performance data. No distinction is made for calculations above or below bubble point conditions. However, for calculations

---

[1] V. Vishal • T.N. Singh: Geologic Carbon Sequestration. Springer International Publishing Switzerland 2016. P 201: 202

below bubble point, the rock and water compressibility values are not important.

For a closed volumetric reservoir (no fluid migration in or out), the original oil-in-place value calculated for different times should agree within a few percent and tend to be constant. However, if there is fluid migration into the reservoir area-that is, water influx from an adjoining aquifer or gas influx from the gas cap-then the value of original oil in place with time should be increasing. None of these values computed assuming depletion drive is true under such conditions and should be disregarded. [1]

6.1.2. OIL IN PLACE AND RECOVERABLE RESERVE BY THE VOLUMETRIC METHOD

The volumetric method of determining oil in place and primary reserve is probably the oldest and most commonly used method. It is perhaps also one of the most abused techniques; therefore, extreme caution and care should be exercised when utilizing it.

Although computation of oil in place and reserve is quite simple and easy to understand, it does require a considerable amount of work and good engineering judgment

---

[1]MIHIR K. SINHA, LARRY R. PADGETT: RESERVOIR ENGINEERING TECHNIQUES USING FORTRAN. D. Reidel Publishing Company 1985. P 41

to arrive at various parameters such as porosity, water saturation, formation volume factor, net sand thickness, extent or size of the reservoir, and the recovery factor (RF). Recovery factor is a function of the prevailing driving mechanism, the reservoir, and the reservoir fluid properties. [1]

Enhanced oil recovery (EOR), sometimes called improved oil recovery, is a term used for tertiary recovery methods in which energy is supplied by injecting substances which are not normally present in the reservoir. The purpose is to increase the recovery factor beyond what can be achieved by primary production methods (pressure depletion) or secondary production (water or natural gas injection), which on the average is of the order of 35 %. Most EOR methods are expensive and on the global scale there has been a clear connection between the oil price and the willingness of the oil companies to start up such measures. Internationally the EOR methods have so far almost exclusively been used on onshore fields and have created significant values for the owners. Offshore application is still in its infancy, but studies predict that a combination of methods technically has the potential for an increase of 15–25 %. [2]

---

[1] MIHIR K. SINHA, LARRY R. PADGETT: RESERVOIR ENGINEERING TECHNIQUES USING FORTRAN. D. Reidel Publishing Company 1985. P 31

Thermal EOR techniques are used to reduce the viscosity of the oil, thereby improving its mobility, and allowing the oil to be more efficiently displaced to the producing wells. This is the most common EOR technique used on onshore reservoirs with oil gravity less than 20°API. Steam or hot water is injected into the reservoir.

This can be done in dedicated injectors (steam or hot water drives) and producing oil from other wells much the same way as with water drives. Alternatively, the steam stimulation and production can be carried out in the same well in a cyclic process called "huff'n puff" in which the steam first soaks the reservoir before it is withdrawn allowing the oil production to take place. A more spectacular method is *in-situ combustion* or fire flooding where heat is generated by igniting a mixture of hydrocarbon gas and oxygen directly in the reservoir. As the fire moves, the burning front pushes ahead a mixture of hot combustion gases, steam and hot water, which in turn reduces oil viscosity and displaces oil toward production wells.

Chemical EOR techniques includes the injection of *polymers* which are long chained

---

([2])Patrick A. Narbel • Jan Petter Hansen Jan R. Lien: Energy Technologies and Economics. Springer International Publishing Switzerland 2014. P 84

organic molecules with high molecular weight, often one thousand or more.

Both biopolymers (e.g. xanthan) or synthetic polymers are used. When injected in water with special chemicals added, the polymer forms a *gel* which resembles a thick soup. This increases the viscosity of the displacing fluid, thereby reducing the mobility ratio M between water and oil to a more favorable value. [1]

Hence, a more efficient volumetric sweep efficiency is achieved and an early water breakthrough can be avoided. The gel formed by polymers can also be used as a blocking agent, sealing off cracks and channels where the displacing fluids may take shortcuts to the producing wells, leaving much oil behind. Use of *surfactants* is another chemical technique. A surfactant acts much the same way as a dish washing detergent which dissolves fat in the washing water. It is a chemical that preferentially adsorbs at an interface, lowering the surface tension or interfacial tension between fluids or between a fluid and a solid. Simply stated, one may say that the water and oil mix and form microemulsions which are more eligible for flow through the pore system of the reservoir rock. The residual oil saturation S_{or} is

---

[1] Patrick A. Narbel • Jan Petter Hansen Jan R. Lien: Energy Technologies and Economics. Springer International Publishing Switzerland 2014. P 85

then reduced, and the microscopic displacement factor *ED* improved. The overall result is a better recovery factor *ER*.

A relatively new chemical EOR technique known as *alkaline surfactant polymer* (ASP) which is a mixture of polymer and surfactant, has successfully been conducted worldwide in recent years. Some ASP floods has been achieving 20 % incremental oil recovery.

Miscible EOR techniques implies the injection of miscible gases into the reservoir. A miscible displacement process maintains reservoir pressure and improves oil displacement because the interfacial tension between oil and water is reduced. Miscible displacement is a major branch of enhanced oil recovery processes. Injected gases include liquefied petroleum gas (LPG), such as propane, methane under high pressure, methane enriched with light hydrocarbons, nitrogen under high pressure, and carbon dioxide (CO_2) under suitable reservoir conditions of temperature and pressure. The fluid most commonly used for miscible displacement is carbon dioxide because it reduces the oil viscosity and is less expensive than liquefied petroleum gas. A special and effective miscible method is called Water-Alternating-Gas (WAG) which has also been applied to offshore fields in the North. This is a process used mostly in CO_2 floods, whereby water injection and gas injection are carried out alternately for periods of time to provide better sweep efficiency and reduce gas channeling from injector to producer.

EOR techniques require use of large amounts of chemicals and therefore represent a substantial *environmental hazard*. Offshore application creates extraordinary challenges related to the handling of back produced EOR chemicals and discharge to sea. These risks need to be assessed, and handling requirements before discharge must be established. It is necessary not only to use those chemicals which are technically most effective, but at the same time select those which have the lowest risk of environmental damage. The economic impact of implementation of EOR techniques can therefore be tremendous both for the operator and the society. [1]

6.1.3. DISPERSED GAS INJECTION PERFORMANCE

The conformance factor e is the fraction of the total net reservoir pore volume that is assumed to be contacted by the injection gas. The injection gas is assumed to be dispersed evenly throughout the conformable portion of the reservoir, and no frontal displacement occurs. Also, gas-oil miscibility is not

---

[1]Patrick A. Narbel • Jan Petter Hansen Jan R. Lien: Energy Technologies and Economics. Springer International Publishing Switzerland 2014. P 85

considered. The production mechanism description can be divided into two regions- namely, conformable and nonconformable portions of the reservoir. The oil from the nonconformable portion of the reservoir is produced by only a depletion or a solution gas drive mechanism and flows into the conformable portion of the reservoir. In the conformable portion of the reservoir, a combination drive-that is, a solution gas drive and dispersed gas injection drive-is envisioned.

The volume of gas injected is provided by the user as a fraction or multiple of the produced gas volume. The series of pressure steps at which the performances are to be calculated as well as the respective fluid properties are provided by the user.

A major problem, however, for the user is to estimate the conformance factor and to determine if the oil from the nonconformable portion of the reservoir is flowing directly into the producing wells. Therefore, selection of these parameters will need considerable prudence and judgement. [1]

6.1.4. Hydrocarbon Recovery and Treatment

Oil recovery technology directly from spillages has improved such that high percentage

[1] MIHIR K. SINHA, LARRY R. PADGETT: RESERVOIR ENGINEERING TECHNIQUES USING FORTRAN. D. Reidel Publishing Company 1985. P 113

efficiency can be achieved. But the recovery efficiency depends upon the nature of the soil, the water course and the nature of the hydrocarbon spilled. Complete recovery/removal of the spilled hydrocarbons is usually not achieved and further treatment of contaminated soil is necessary. Disposal of land contaminated by hydrocarbons to landfill is now more restricted as to the hydrocarbon content, from higher standards/lower allowed concentration limits, and recognition that the problem is not being addressed but moved 'along the line' for other people to deal with the problem at a later time. The soil volumes to be treated can be very high. Previous minor/moderate contamination of a development site might require removal of the top 0.5 m, or up to 1 m, of the site topsoil, very large volumes to be lifted, transported and disposed in a safe manner. Alternative on-site treatment methods can be used – incineration to destroy hydrocarbons present in soil can be destructive of the soil and expensive of fuel to operate; solvent extraction is effective but care must be taken to avoid extra emissions arising from the solvent used. Biological treatment of hydrocarbon-contaminated soil can be effective for appropriate combinations of soil type and grade/type of hydrocarbon but requires time and space to be effective.

Contaminated groundwater is recovered using oil/water separators in the first instance, as in drainage sumps for water run-off from hard surfaces/hard standing, specified in the Building Regulation site consent. The efficiency of simple oil/water separators does not give sufficiently acceptable purity for the separated water and it must be treated further. Techniques for further water purification include (i) relatively gentle physical separation using tank settlement or plate impingement separators, (ii) more active physical treatment such as fine filtration, sedimentation settling, flocculation by settlement-promoting additives or air/froth flotation, or (iii) biological treatments using biofilters of various designs such as reed beds, air pumped through aerated ponds of the water being treated, or very intensive treatment by the activated sludge process. After further slow settlement, high quality water effluent from these treatments can be discharged to a water course. [1]

6.1.5. FUTURE RESERVOIR PERFORMANCE

Extrapolation of characteristic production decline trends from past performance is used to predict future performance of a producing well or reservoir. The historical data must represent unrestricted (capacity) production. The basis of extrapolation is the assumption that the future behavior of a

---

[1]Stefan Orszulik: Environmental Technology in the Oil Industry. Third edition. Springer International Publishing Switzerland 2016. P 403: 404

well/reservoir will be governed by the past trend or mathematical relation that represents its past performance.

Regression analysis technique is applied to determine the optimal values of the characteristic parameters (decline constant and exponent) of the generalized decline curve equation. [1]

6.1.6. POLYMER FLOOD PERFORMANCE

Although the theoretical basis for increased oil recovery by polymer flood is sound, actual field performance is usually lower than that predicted by analytical solutions or laboratory experiment. Empirical data suggest that the addition of polymer improves sweep by 1% for every 10% that the primary/secondary sweep is less than 100%; that is, the recoveries are inversely dependent on the effectiveness of the waterflood sweep.

The estimate provided by this program will indicate relatively good or improved flood performance when waterflood results are poor. Conversely, however, the estimate will show relatively insignificant performance improvement when the waterflood performance has been good. [2]

---

[1]MIHIR K. SINHA, LARRY R. PADGETT: RESERVOIR ENGINEERING TECHNIQUES USING FORTRAN. D. Reidel Publishing Company 1985. P 71
[2]MIHIR K. SINHA, LARRY R. PADGETT:

6.1.7. Chemical Recovery

Some liquids have a higher affinity than others to adhere to solid surfaces. When two liquids are in contact with a common solid surface, one of the two liquids (the one with the higher adhesion affinity) will spread over the surface at the expense of the other. The solid surface is then identified as wettable by that liquid. Most reservoir rocks are wetted by water than by oil and are, therefore, identified as water-wet rocks. Such conditions are favorable for displacing oil by water. There are situations, however, where the reservoir rocks are oil-wet. In these cases, water would not be able to displace the oil. Reservoir engineers and surface chemistry scientists have developed methods in which chemicals are used to change the wettability of the rock for effective water-flooding operations. These methods are known as the chemical recovery methods. The two most common chemical recovery methods are surfactant flooding and caustic flooding.

In surfactant flooding, a slug of water–surfactant solution is first injected through the injection well into the formation. This is followed by injection of ordinary water as in regular water-flooding operations. The surfactant ahead of the floodwater causes changes in the interfacial tension and mobilizes

---

RESERVOIR ENGINEERING TECHNIQUES USING FORTRAN. D. Reidel Publishing Company 1985. P 147

the oil that would otherwise adhere to the surface of the rock. Thus, the displacement of the oil by the floodwater becomes possible. Again, adding polymers to the water to create favorable mobility conditions could increase the flooding effectiveness. In this case, the method can be called surfactant–polymer flooding.

Caustic flooding is essentially a surfactant flooding, with the surfactant being generated within the reservoir rather than being injected. The method is applicable in situations where the reservoir oil contains high concentrations of natural acids, which can react with alkaline to produce surfactants. The most common approach is to inject a slug of caustic soda (NaOH) solution ahead of the floodwater. The alkaline reacts with the acids in the oil to in situ produce surfactants. Then, the process is converted into a surfactant-flooding process. This method is less expensive than the regular surfactant-flooding process.

6.1.8. Miscible Recovery

In miscible recovery, a slug of a substance that is miscible in the reservoir oil is injected into the reservoir at pressures high enough to achieve good miscibility. This is then followed by water injection. The process has been used with carbon dioxide, rich natural gas, nitrogen, flue gases, and light hydrocarbon liquids as the miscible fluid. Miscible flooding could achieve very high recovery factors. [1]

6.1.9. Thermal Recovery

Heavy oil reservoirs present a unique production problem. The high viscosity of the oil makes it difficult, and in some cases impossible, to produce the oil, even with the aforementioned improved recovery methods. The best method to mobilize the oil is to heat the formation to reduce the oil viscosity. When heating is used in recovering the oil, the recovery method is called thermal recovery. The three most common thermal recovery methods are steam stimulation, steam flooding, and in situ combustion.

In the steam stimulation method steam is injected into the producing well for a specified period of time (normally more than a month); then, the well is shut off for another period of time (normally a few days). The injected steam heats up the surrounding formation, causing significant reduction in oil viscosity. The well is then put on production for a period of time until the oil flow declines. The process is then repeated through the same cycle of injection, shutting off, and production. This process is also known as the Hugh and Pugh method.

---

[1]Hussein K. Abdel-Aal Mohamed A. Aggour Mohamed A. Fahim: Petroleum and Gas Field Processing. Second Edition. Taylor & Francis Group, LLC. 2016. P 23: 24

Steam flooding is similar to the water-flooding process, except that steam is used instead of water. The steam is injected into an injection well to reduce the oil viscosity while the condensed steam (hot water) displaces the oil toward the producing wells.

In the in-situ combustion process, air is injected into the formation through an injection well under conditions that initiate ignition of the oil within the nearby formation. The combustion zone creates a front of distilled oil, steam, and gases. Continued air injection drives the combustion front toward the producing wells. The combination of heating and displacement by the steam, gases, and condensed liquids enhances the recovery of the oil. [1]

6.1.10. Pressure Maintenance

As oil is produced, the reservoir pressure declines at a rate that depends on the reservoir drive mechanism, the strength of that drive, and the amount of oil produced. Solution gas drive reservoirs experience the highest rate of pressure decline, followed by the gas cap drive reservoirs, with the water drive reservoirs being the least affected. The decrease in reservoir pressure reduces the ability of the formation to produce oil. The loss of

---

[1]Hussein K. Abdel-Aal Mohamed A. Aggour Mohamed A. Fahim: Petroleum and Gas Field Processing. Second Edition. Taylor & Francis Group, LLC. 2016. P 24: 25

productivity becomes very severe if the reservoir pressure drops below the bubble point pressure.

One way of maintaining a high reservoir pressure to maintain productivity and increase recovery is to inject a fluid into the reservoir at such quantities and pressure that it will keep the reservoir pressure at the desired high level. Depending on the type of reservoir, pressure maintenance may be achieved by either the injection of water through wells drilled at the periphery of the reservoir or the injection of gas at the top of the reservoir. [1]

6.1.11. Water Flooding

In water flooding, injection wells are drilled between the oil producing wells in a specific regular pattern. For example, for the 5-spot flooding pattern, one injection well is drilled between and at equal distances from four producing wells. Water is injected into the injection well to drive (push) the oil toward the four producers. Simulations of the process are usually made before implementation to determine the optimum well spacing, or pattern, and the injection rate and pressure to achieve efficient displacement of oil by the injected water. Water-flooding operations are always associated with a high water cut in the produced

---

[1]Hussein K. Abdel-Aal Mohamed A. Aggour Mohamed A. Fahim: Petroleum and Gas Field Processing. Second Edition. Taylor & Francis Group, LLC. 2016. P 23

fluid. The process continues until the oil production rate becomes too low for economic operation.

Since the water viscosity is lower than the oil viscosity, water may finger through the oil and reach the producing well prematurely, bypassing a significant amount of oil that would be very difficult to recover. Engineers have to be careful in determining the injection rate for the specific reservoir and rock and fluid properties to avoid water fingering. Water flooding could be improved if the water viscosity were altered to become higher than the oil viscosity. This would create more favorable mobility conditions, make the oil–water interface more stable, and avoid fingering. This is achieved by adding certain polymers to the injection water. This is known as polymer flooding. [1]

6.2. Intensification and Reversal of the Oil Recovery

More than 90 percent of US crude oil was produced from reservoirs located in nine states during the period 1965–74. Of this, nearly two- thirds was produced in Texas and Louisiana. The remaining one-third came from California, Oklahoma, Wyoming, New Mexico, Alaska, Kansas, and Mississippi. Studying the

---

[1] Hussein K. Abdel-Aal Mohamed A. Aggour Mohamed A. Fahim: Petroleum and Gas Field Processing. Second Edition. Taylor & Francis Group, LLC. 2016. P 23

trend of average oil recovery in the United States and in the principal oil-producing states, in conjunction with the long-run investment per barrel, is one possible way of examining the actual emerging conditions that led to the formation of the present cost structure in the oil industry. The identification of decline, either in the trend of oil recovery from the old oil fields or in the rate of new oil discoveries, in conjunction with the long-term cost of oil associated with these spheres of production during the period of 1971–74, reveals which area actually regulates the restructured industry's market value and prices.

    A comparison of these trends requires calculation of the average oil production per well for the above-mentioned major US oil-producing states for 1965, 1971, and 1974. But the average of these averages does not represent the true average, without assigning appropriate weights, such as the actual production shares of these individual states. The comparison of the average oil recovery and corresponding shares of oil production for the US oil-producing states for the period of 1965–74 can be found in Bina. These findings show that the conditions of capital investments and production during 1971–74 were entirely different from those in the previous period. The increasing volume of capital investments on the existing oil fields, and the production of reserves by way of intensification, extension, and enhanced recovery methods, led to the subsequent decline of average oil recovery per well in the aging US oil fields.

One has to bear in mind that this decline is not simply incidental to the oil crisis of 1973–74. The crisis is, in fact, both the symptom of and the social mechanism for the generalization of production conditions under these newly emerged circumstances. The magnitudes of the cost of production and of the individual value produced for the aging US oil fields, due to the intensification of production, had significantly increased. Being the least productive of all US oil fields, their corresponding newly formed individual value has become the social value of the entire industry. [1]

6.3. Improved Petroleum Recovery

The natural reservoir drive mechanisms described in Section 1.5.2 normally result in low recovery factors. In fact, if reservoirs were produced solely by the natural driving forces, very poor recoveries would be obtained. The specific rock and fluids properties and the forces that control the movements of the fluids within the reservoir are responsible for such poor recoveries. Petroleum recovery by

---

[1] Cyrus Bina: A Prelude to the Foundation of Political Economy. PALGRAVE MACMILLAN. 2013. P 28: 29

these natural drive mechanisms is called primary recovery.

In order to achieve recoveries higher than the primary recovery, we must intervene into the reservoir to artificially control, or alter, the natural driving forces and the rock and fluids properties. Reservoir engineers have developed, and continued research is being conducted for further developments, refinement, and improvement, and various techniques to achieve higher than primary recoveries. Some techniques involve supplementing the natural driving force by injecting high-pressure fluids into the reservoir. Other techniques aim at changing the fluids or rock properties to enhance the mobility of the petroleum fluids and suppress the forces that hinder their movements. All such techniques are known as enhanced recovery methods or improved recovery methods. A brief description of some of the improved recovery methods follows. [1]

6.4. Major differences between oil and gas field development

The main differences between oil and gas field development are associated with

_ the economics of transporting gas

---

[1] Hussein K. Abdel-Aal Mohamed A. Aggour Mohamed A. Fahim: Petroleum and Gas Field Processing. Second Edition. Taylor & Francis Group, LLC. 2016. P 22

_ the market for gas

_ product specifications

_ the efficiency of turning gas into energy.

Per unit of energy generated, the transportation of gas is significantly more expensive than transporting oil, due to the volumes required to yield the same energy. In other words, the energy density of gas is low compared to oil. On a calorific basis approximately 6000 scf of gas is equivalent to one barrel (5.6 scf) of oil. The compression costs of transporting gas at sufficient pressure to make transportation more economic are also high. This means that unless there are sufficiently large

quantities of gas in the reservoir to take advantage of economies of scale, development may be uneconomic.

For an offshore field requiring significant infrastructure for development, recoverable volumes of less than 0.5 trillion scf (Tcf) are typically uneconomic to develop. This would equate to an oil field with recoverable reserves of approximately 80 MMstb. If close to existing offshore infrastructure, this threshold is closer to 50 Bcf.

For the above reasons, gas is typically economic to develop only if it can be used locally, that is if a local demand exists. The exception to this is where a sufficient quantity of gas exists to provide the economy of scale to make transportation of gas or liquefied gas attractive. As a guide, approximately 5 Tcf of recoverable gas would be required to justify building a liquefied natural gas (LNG) plant. Globally there are around 30 such plants, but an example would be the LNG plant in Malaysia which liquefies gas and transports it by refrigerated tanker to Japan. The investment capital required for an LNG plant is very large; typically, in the order of $5 billion.

Whereas a 'spot market' has always existed for oil, gas sales traditionally require a contract to be agreed between the producer and a customer. This forms an important part of gas field development planning, since the price agreed between producer and customer will vary, and will depend on the quantity supplied, the plateau length and the flexibility of supply. Whereas oil price is approximately the same across the globe, gas prices can vary very significantly (by a factor of two or more) from region to region.

When a customer agrees to purchase gas, product quality is specified in terms of the calorific value of the gas, measured by the Wobbe Index (WI) (MJ/m3 or Btu/scf), the hydrocarbon dew point and the water dew point, and the fraction of other gases such as N_2, CO_2, H_2S. The WI specification ensures that the gas the customer receives has a predictable calorific value and hence predictable burning characteristics. If the gas becomes lean, less energy is released, and if the gas becomes too rich there is a risk that the gas burners 'flame out'. Water and hydrocarbon dew points (the pressure and temperature at which liquids start to drop out of the gas) are specified to ensure that over the range of temperature and pressure at which the gas is handled by the customer, no liquids will drop out (these could cause possible slugging, corrosion and/or hydrate formation).

H_2S is undesirable because of its toxicity and corrosive properties. CO_2 can cause corrosion in the presence of water, and N_2 simply reduces the calorific value of the gas as it is inert. [1]

6.5. Enhance shale resources

In past years, the supply of shale resources has increased rapidly throughout the North America and the world. However, in the shale gas well, gas rate decreases rapidly after few years of production. Consequently, interest of enhanced gas recovery (EGR) for shale gas reservoir is growing recently. In a shale reservoir, methane (CH4) is adsorbed on surface of the matrix particle or natural fracture face and

[1]Frank Jahn, Mark Cook and Mark Graham: HYDROCARBON EXPLORATION AND PRODUCTION. 2ND EDITION. Elsevier B.V. 2008. P 210: 212

stored in matrix and fracture pore as free gas. Several researches showed that the affinity of carbon dioxide (CO_2) sorption to the shale reservoir is larger than that of CH_4 under the subsurface conditions and depending on the thermal maturity of organic materials. Furthermore, CO_2 injection is important in shale gas reservoir for not only enhanced CH_4 production but also the storage of CO_2. Stronger affinity of CO_2 to the shale reservoir could initiate mechanisms to displace CH_4 existed originally and to adsorb the CO_2 introduced into the shale gas environment. The CO_2 is also could be stored in some portion of the pore volume as non-adsorbed CO_2, especially where hydraulic fracturing has enhanced injectivity.

Although CO_2 injection in shale gas reservoir has not been commercialized yet, several researchers have investigated this subject. Attempts have been made to study the feasibility of CO_2 injection in the Middle and upper Devonian black shale.

Schepers et al. (2009) described the reservoir modeling and history matching of a Devonian gas shale play in eastern Kentucky and its potential for CO_2 enhanced gas recovery and storage. Well production was history matched by applying an automated process. Finally, several CO_2 injection scenarios with huff-n-puff and continuous injection were reviewed to evaluate the enhanced gas recovery potential and to assess the CO2 storage capacity of these shale reservoirs. They concluded that the full-field continuous CO2 injection seems to be of potential success, allowing injection of 300 tons over a period of one and a half month and showing a significant gain in the recovery. In addition, depending upon the thickness considered, half to the total volume injected is being sequestered. However, the huff-and-puff scenario does not seem to be a good option for that specific reservoir, generating no enhanced gas recovery due to the CO2 being reproduced very quickly during the puff periods. Even trying longer soaking periods did not seem to improve the recovery.

Liu et al. (2013) focused on CO2 storage in Devonian and Mississippian New Albany shale gas play in terms of injectivity, storage capacity, sequestration effectiveness, and its impact on CH4 production. They showed over 95 % of injected CO2 is effectively sequestered instantaneously with gas adsorption being the dominate storage mechanism. Microscale studies using optical, nuclear, and petrophysical techniques also support the interpretation that gas shales have abundant nano-scale pores in organic matter that allow CO2 storage through gas adsorption.

Fathi and Akkutlu (2013) presented new mathematical model based on the Maxwell-Stefan formulation for simulations of multi-component transport between CO2 and CH4 in shale reservoirs. The approach considered competitive transport and adsorption effect in the organic micropores of the shale during CO2 injection.

Focus of their paper was to develop a new triple-porosity single-permeability flow simulation model which is based on a new kinetic approach for the description of gas release from the organic micropores into the inorganic macropores and fractures.

It is shown that the surface diffusion of the adsorbed molecules in the micropores is an important mechanism of transport during the CO2 enhanced shale gas recovery since it leads to important counter diffusion and competitive adsorption effects.

Because CO2 injection technique for shale formations is still in its very preliminary stage in spite of these previous researches, study for more accurate simulation model of CO2 injection in shale reservoir is needed. used gas well data from Barnett Shale in order to model the shale reservoir more accurately. Using this field data, history matching is performed and reservoir and fracture properties of shale gas reservoir for CO2 injection simulation are obtained.

Comprehensive reservoir simulation models are presented to investigate effective CO2 injection strategy considering reservoir and fracture properties. Sensitivity analysis for either enhanced CH4 recovery or CO2 storage is conducted to investigate the critical parameters that control CO2-EGR process and CO2 storage, respectively. In following section, this work is introduced in detail, which is important for better understanding of basic mechanisms and proper design of CO2 injection in order to enhance CH4 recovery and CO2 storage.

Although dissolution, residual, and mineral trapping are known as the general trapping mechanisms for immobilization of CO2 in geological media, in shale gas reservoir, adsorption trapping is a dominant mechanism for CO2 storage due to affinity of CO2 to the organic shale. In order to calculate competitive multi-component adsorption/desorption in the model, extended Langmuir isotherm, which has been proven to present a reasonable correlation of the CH4 and CO2 binary gas sorption, is applied given bellow

$$\omega_i = \frac{\omega_{i,\max} B_i y_{ig} p}{1 + p \sum_j B_j y_{jg}},$$

where ω_i is the moles of adsorbed component i per unit mass of rock, $\omega_{i,\max}$ the maximum moles of adsorbed component i per unit mass of rock, Bi the parameter for Langmuir isotherm relation, y_{ig} the molar fraction of adsorbed component i in the gas phase, and p the pressure.

Dissolution trapping is considered by gas solubility represented by Henry's law. Dissolution of the component i in the reservoir fluid is calculated by Henry's law as Follows

$$y_{iw} H_i = f_{iw},$$

where y_{iw} is the mole fraction of component i in the aqueous phase, Hi the Henry's constant of component i, and f_{iw} the fugacity of component i in the aqueous phase.

The aqueous phase and the gaseous phase are assumed in thermodynamic equilibrium so that f_{iw} is equal to the fugacity of component i in the gas phase fig. fig is computed from Peng and Robinson (1976) equation of state. The Henry's constants Hi are calculated by below equation

$$\ln H_i = \ln H_i^* + \frac{\bar{V}_i(p - p^*)}{RT},$$

where Hi * is the Henry's constant for component i at reference pressure p*, _Vi the partial molar volume of component i, p* the reference pressure, R the universal gas constant, and T the temperature.

Due to ultra-low permeability of shale matrix, diffusion in the reservoir is significantly important. Especially, when CO2 is introduced in the reservoir, effect of molecular diffusion between CH4 and CO2 should be considered. Sigmund (1976a, b) conducted experiments for various gases to investigate the binary diffusion coefficient.

From the results of the experiments, following polynomial was obtained by fitting with the observed values.

$$D_{ij} = \frac{\rho^0 D_{ij}^0}{\rho}\left(0.99589 + 0.096016\rho_r - 0.22035\rho_r^2 + 0.032874\rho_r^3\right),$$

where D_{ij} is the binary diffusion coefficient between component i and j in the mixture, $\rho^0 D^0{}_{ij}$ the zero-pressure limit of the density-diffusivity product, ρ the molar density of the diffusing mixture, and ρ_r the reduced density. From the above equation for binary diffusion coefficient, the diffusion coefficient of component i in the mixture can be computed as follow,

$$D_i = \frac{1 - y_i}{\sum_{j \neq i} y_i D_{ij}^{-1}},$$

where D_i is the diffusion coefficient of component i in the mixture and y_i the mole fraction of component i. With this calculation, competitive diffusion between CH4 and CO2 was modeled.

Previous studies showed that linear-elastic model cannot solely describe the geo mechanical effects of shale gas reservoirs. Meanwhile, in order to consider the change of reservoir conductivity, pressure-dependent permeability was presented in several researches. Therefore, the deformation of shale reservoir is modeled by stress-dependent correlations coupled with linear-elastic model. Exponential correlation is used to calculate these stress-dependent porosity and permeability. Experimental coefficients are obtained from Cho et al. (2013).

In order to analyze the realistic effects of CO2 injection in shale gas reservoir, numerical model of shale gas reservoir was generated based on properties from history matching. Field data of Barnett Shale reproduced from Anderson

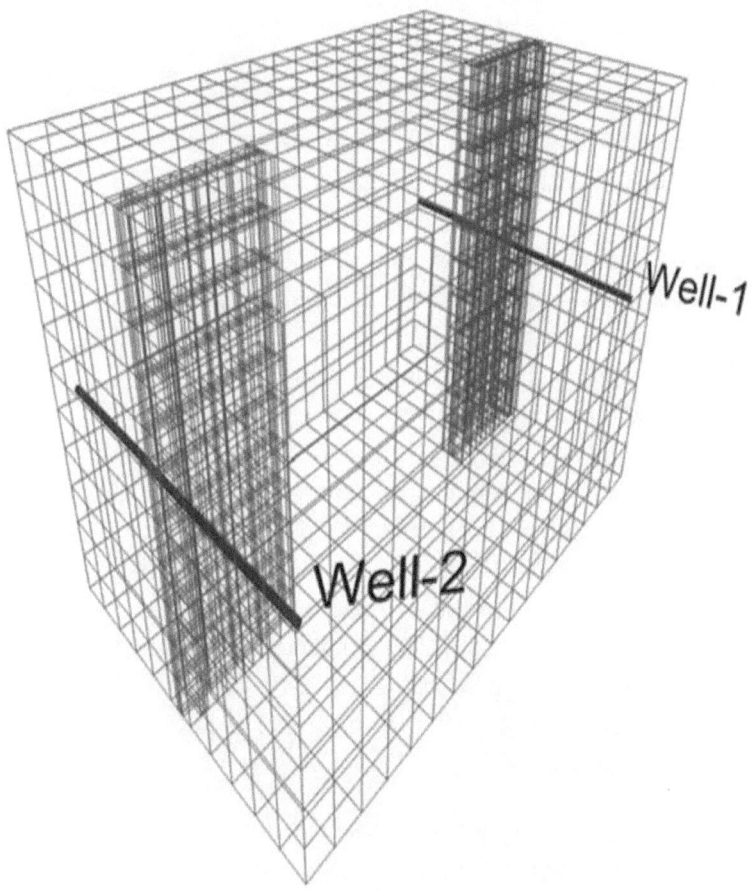

were used to perform history matching. Using the results of history matching, the segment of reservoir, which is simplified for computational efficiency, was generated with two hydraulically fractured horizontal well.

The size of the segment is 330 × 510 × 330 ft^3. In this model, dual porosity dual permeability model was considered to characterize the matrix and natural fracture system in shale gas reservoir. The horizontal wells are located at the center of the reservoir and hydraulic fractures are located at the center of the each well. Local grid refinement (LGR) technique is used to model the thin block assigned with the properties of hydraulic fracture. Height of the hydraulic fractures is same as net pay which shows fully penetrated reservoir. It is assumed that properties of hydraulic fracture are constant along the fracture and have finite conductivity. To analyze the effects of the geo mechanical model, exponential correlation is considered coupled with linear-elastic model. In the simulation scenario, at first, two horizontal wells are produced for five years. Then, in the well 2, CO_2 is injected while well 1 continues to produce. After five years, CO_2 injector well 2 is shut-in and well 1 is produced for 40 years.

In order to investigate the effects of CO_2 injection for EGR, gas recovery from the model with and without CO_2 injection is presented in Fig. This graph shows that recovery of each model with and without CO_2 injection is 51.1 and 38.7 % so that increase of recovery caused by CO_2 flooding is 12.4 % at the end of the production. Figures show cumulative gas moles and gas mole rate of CH_4 and CO_2 with and without CO_2 injection observed in the production well 1. Figure indicates that about 98 % of the produced gas in the well 1 is CH4 and

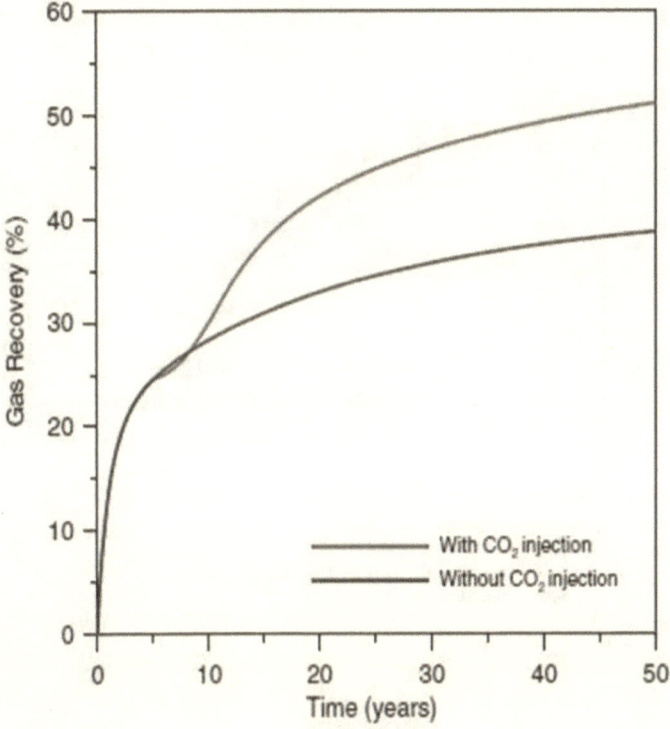

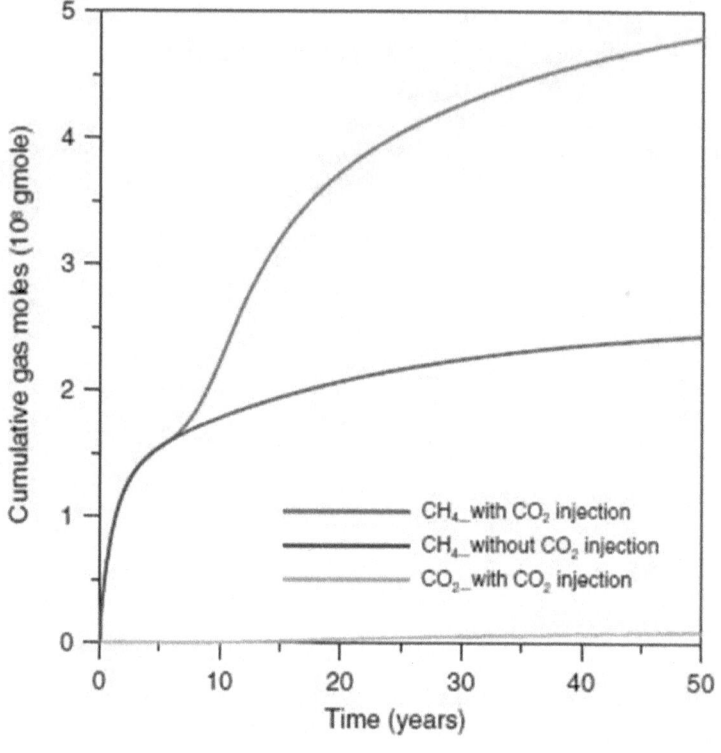

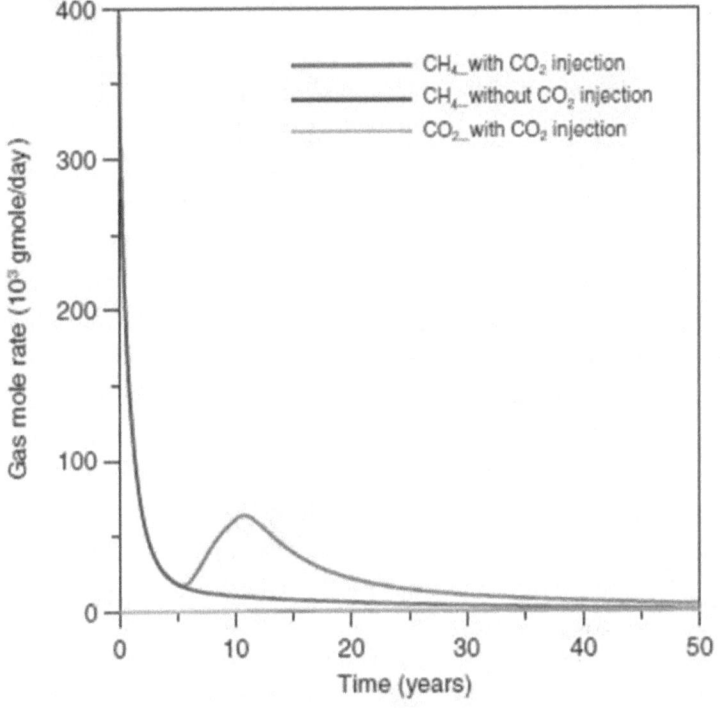

only about 2 % of the produced gas is CO_2. Increasing CH_4 production caused by CO_2 injection is observed approximately 1 year after injection started. CO_2 breakthrough is observed 3 years after injection started in the well 1 but production rate remains extremely low. In Fig, the peak of CH_4 is shown approximately 1 year after the shut-in and it is 5 times the CH_4 rate of model without CO_2 injection.

The Figure shows moles of injected, stored, and produced CO_2 in the shale reservoir. In this figure, about 96 % of total injected CO_2

is stored in the reservoir and only about 4 % is produced from the production well at the end of the production. The Figure provides the classification of injected CO_2 in the shale reservoir based on the states of CO_2 such as super-critical, adsorbed, dissolved, and produced CO_2. The CO_2 stored in the reservoir exists as a super-critical phase, adsorption trapping, and dissolution trapping of 45.8, 46.5, and 3.6 %, respectively at the end of the production. Among these states of CO_2, super-critical phase is mobile but adsorption and dissolution states are immobile because they are trapped in the surface of matrix and connate water respectively. Directly after the end of CO_2 injection, the amount of super-critical CO_2 is higher than that of adsorbed CO_2.

However, as time goes on, super-critical CO_2 spreads to the reservoir and amount of super-critical CO_2 decreases due to increase of adsorption and dissolution trapping.

The Figure presents adsorbed moles of the CH_4 and the CO_2 with and without considering the multi-component adsorption mechanism. Solid and dashed lines indicate the amount of CH_4 and CO_2 adsorption, respectively. Red and blue lines

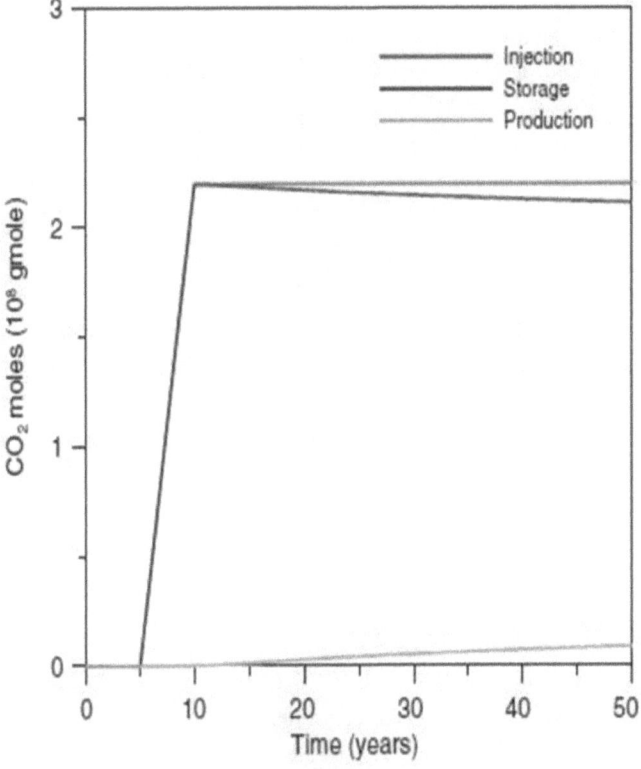

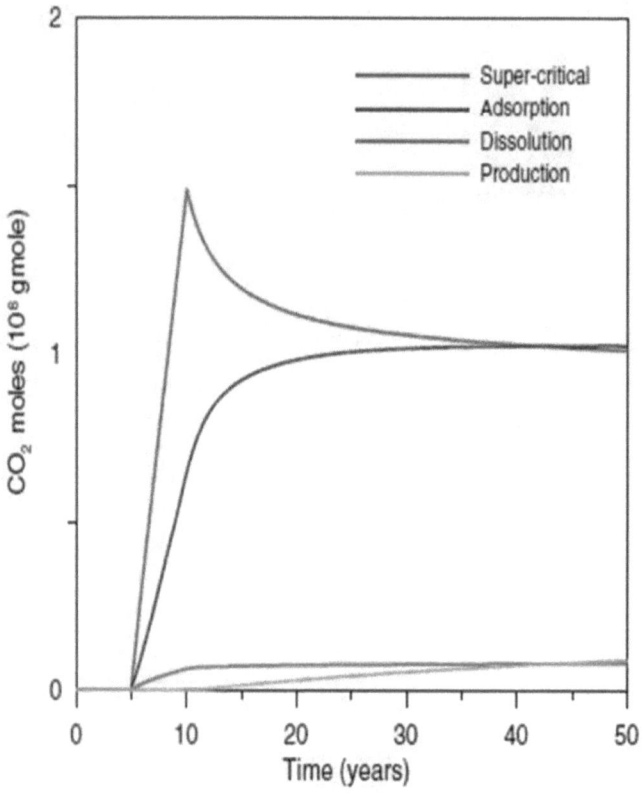

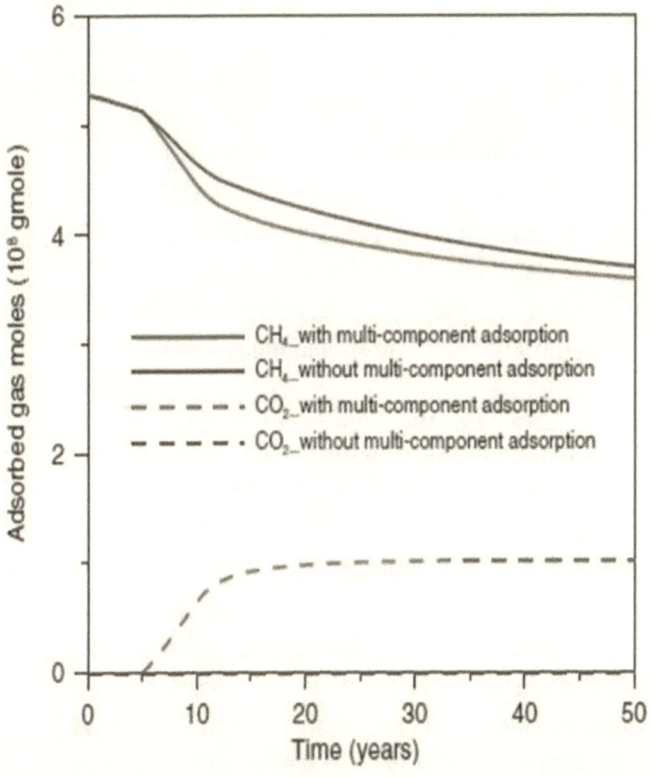

indicate whether the multi-component adsorption is considered or not. In the model without the multi-component adsorption, the CO2 injection only causes the effect of pressurizing the reservoir and the CO2 is not adsorbed in the shale reservoir. On the other hand, in the model with the multi-component adsorption, desorption of the CH4 is activated by competitive sorption with the CO2 which is preferentially adsorbed over CH4 with a ratio up to 5:1 based on laboratory and theoretical calculations (Nuttall 2010). In Fig desorption of CH_4 is higher in the model with the multi-component adsorption. The Figure shows that schematic view of the CO_2 adsorption in the reservoir. the Figure a through c indicate gmole per cubic feet of CO_2 adsorption after 10, 30, 50 years, respectively. After injection stops, while production continues for 40 years, the CO_2 migrates to the production well so that the adsorption of CO_2 spreads to the reservoir.

Mole fraction of CH_4 and CO_2 is compared in the model with and without mechanism of the molecular diffusion. These values are measured from the point A of the reservoir model shown in Fig. In Fig. solid and dashed lines indicate the mole fraction of CH_4 and CO_2 and red and blue lines indicate whether the molecular diffusion is considered or not. Figure shows that the mole fraction of CH_4 decreases about 10 % and that of CO_2 increases about 10 % due to the effect of molecular diffusion computed by Sigmund correlation (1976a, b).

Figure also presents schematic view of the CH_4 mol fraction in the reservoir at the end of the production. Figure a which shows the model considering molecular diffusion presents more widely-spread CO_2 in the reservoir compared with Fig.b. Because of ultra-low permeability of shale reservoir, effect of diffusion is higher than conventional reservoirs so that it should be considered in the CO2 injection model of shale reservoir.

Geo mechanical effects are also important in the shale reservoir (Cho et al. 2013).

In order to calculate the geo mechanical effects, stress-dependent porosity and permeability coupled with linear-elastic model is applied in this model. Exponential correlations are used to compute the stress-dependent properties. Figure shows the change of natural fracture permeability in the model with and without CO2 injection. In first five years, permeability decreases rapidly due to the decrease of pressure during production. After injection begins, natural fracture permeability increases until the shut-in of injection well and decreases again. Due to the pressurizing effect caused by injection of CO2, average pressure increases shown as Fig. so that permeability increases depending on the stress-dependent correlation.

Increment of porosity and permeability caused by geo mechanical model has a positive effect on the CO2 injection in the shale reservoir.

Shale gas reservoirs show high uncertainty because of inestimable reservoir and fracture properties. Although several sensitivity studies for CO2-EGR were performed, there are no results for the CO2 storage in shale formations. In this study, sensitivity analysis was performed for the both CH4 recovery and the CO2 storage. Especially, in stored CO2, adsorption and dissolution states are immobile because they are trapped in the surface of matrix and connate water and they are important for the CO2 storage due to stability. Therefore, sensitivity analysis for the trapped CO2 is also conducted.

Figures provide results of sensitivity analysis for the objective functions of cumulative produced moles of CH4, stored moles of CO2 in reservoir, and trapped moles of CO2. In this study, uncertain parameters considered for sensitivity analysis are porosity of matrix and natural fractures, permeability of matrix, natural fractures, and hydraulic fractures, hydraulic fracture height, hydraulic fracture half-length, Langmuir volume, and Langmuir pressure. Effects of parameters which show high influence to each sensitivity analysis were presented in Figs for the CO2-EGR, matrix porosity, natural fracture permeability and height are significantly of importance. It shows that effects of EGR increase with high fracture conductivity. On the other hand, for the CO2 storage, influence of uncertain parameters are small compared with the result of EGR. In this case, hydraulic fracture half-length is most important and dominant parameter. For the CO_2 trapping, Langmuir constants are main parameters.

Therefore, these parameters should be mainly considered to inject CO_2 in the shale gas reservoir for each objective.

Recently, enhanced oil recovery (EOR) in shale oil reservoir is also concentrated as well as EGR in shale gas reservoir. Tovar et al. (2014) presented experimental results on the use of CO_2 as an EOR agent in preserved, rotary sidewall reservoir core samples with negligible permeability. The results of this investigation support CO_2 as a promising EOR agent for shale oil reservoir. Oil recovery was estimated to be between 18 and 55 % of OOIP. They provided a detailed description of the experimental set up and procedures. The analysis of the x-ray computed tomography images revealed saturation changes within the shale core as a result of CO_2 injection. Chen et al. (2014), Yu et al. (2014b), Wan and Sheng (2015) presented simulation study for EOR in shale oil reservoir. In spite of these previous studies, research of EGR and EOR in shale reservoir is still lacking. In the future, for stable production in shale reservoirs, more research of this area is needed. [1]

---

[1] Kun Sang Lee • Tae Hong Kim: Integrative Understanding of Shale Gas Reservoirs. 2016. P 105: 118

7. CONVENTIONAL PETROLEUM

At the present time, several countries are recognized as producers of petroleum and have available reserves. These available reserves have been defined, but not quite in the manner outlined earlier. For example, on a worldwide basis the produced conventional crude oil is estimated to be approximately 784 billion (784 * 10^9) bbl with approximately 836 billion bbl remaining as reserves. It is also estimated that there are 180 billion bbl which remain to be discovered with approximately 1 trillion (1 * 10^{12}) bbl yet-to-be -produced. The annual depletion rate is estimated to be 2.6%.

The United States is an oil-based culture, one of the largest importers of petroleum and, as the imports of crude oil into the United States continue to rise, it is interesting, perhaps frightening, that projections made in 1990 are remarkably close to the current import scenarios. The United States now imports approximately 65% of its daily crude oil (and crud e oil product) requirements. As recent events have shown, there seems to be little direct ion in terms of stability of supply or any measure of self-sufficiency in liquid fuels precursors, other than resorting to military action. This is particularly important for the United States refineries since a disrupt ion in supply could cause major shortfalls in feedstock avail ability.

In addition, the crude oils available today to the refinery are quite different in composition and properties to those available some 50 years ago. The current crud e oils are somewhat heavier, as they have higher proportions of nonvolatile (asphaltic) constituent s. In fact, by the standard s of yesteryear, many of the crude oils currently in use would have been classified as heavy feedstock, bearing in mind that they may not approach the definitions used today for heavy crude oil. Changes in feedstock character, such as this tendency to heavier material s, require adjustments to refinery operations to handle these heavier crude oils to reduce the amount of coke formed during processing and to balance the overall product slate. [1]

7.1. Reserves–Production Ratio

Reserves–production ratio (RPR) is the measure of reserves life and is the ratio of recoverable oil reserves to current oil production rate. It is an important ratio for formulating future strategies and indicates how long the reserves would last at the current production rate. A country with high RPR is in a comfortable position in respect of energy availability.

---

[1]James G. Speight: The Chemistry and Technology of Petroleum. FOURTH EDITION. Taylor & Francis Group, LLC. 2007. P 107:108

On the other hand, a low RPR signifies its vulnerability to outside shock and limited options for maneuverability.

The economic prosperity of a country is closely related to its energy consumption level.

The higher the per capita energy consumption, the higher is the economic prosperity of the country. It is desirable to increase oil production capacity for all-round growth of the country. But increased oil production would result in early depletion of reserves, and if produced at a faster rate beyond the optimum level, it would affect the health of the reservoir, which would be detrimental in the long run. In order to strike a balance between the economic growth of a country and the reserves life, the RPR shall be kept at an optimum level. The desired value of RPR varies from country to country depending on the quantum or availability of reserves, production capacity, and consumption rate. For the instant case/country, the desired RPR is 20 years, which is indicative of many other countries. [1]

7.2. Reservoir Management

The aspects of reservoir management are numerous and involve extensive and

[1] Sanjib Chowdhury: Optimization and Business Improvement Studies in Upstream Oil and Gas Industry. John Wiley & Sons, Inc. 2016. P 297:298

complicated studies. In simple terms, however, the role of reservoir management is to specify specific producing strategies that will control the movements of the various fluids within the reservoir in order to achieve maximum recovery of the hydrocarbon materials while minimizing the production of undesired fluids. The production strategies may include assignment of production rates to individual wells in the field, shutting off certain wells for a specific duration, drilling of new wells at specific locations, and implementing specific pressure maintenance or improved recovery operations. The importance of reservoir management has been recognized in recent years. This led to the formation of specialized groups and departments for reservoir management in most major oil companies. [1]

7.3. Economic Balance in Oil Fields (Optimization)

The recovery of oil from underground, or offshore, reservoirs is a good application of the principle of economic balance. The problem is one of determining the optimum number of wells to drill, and the accurate spacing of these wells, to get maximum profit. The following considerations highlight the subject.

---

[1] Hussein K. Abdel-Aal Mohamed A. Aggour Mohamed A. Fahim: Petroleum and Gas Field Processing. Second Edition. Taylor & Francis Group, LLC. 2016. P 22

The greater the number of wells, the larger will be the ultimate recovery, provided that the recovery rate does not exceed the "most efficient engineering rate." However, the most efficient engineering rate (economic balance) does not necessarily mean the optimum rate for maximum profits. Economic balance, therefore, consists of a balance of greater fixed costs for a larger number of wells drilled plus usually higher operating costs for higher production rates against greater ultimate recovery from the larger number of wells.

Thus, the principle of economic balance in the oil fields is to drill as many wells as possible and needed within fixed costs and operating cost limits relative to the greatest ultimate recovery in terms of the realizable value (sales value) for the recovery. There is an upper limit to the number of wells that can be drilled, however, because of technical considerations. In other words, greater fixed costs plus higher operating costs must be considered when increasing the number of wells to be drilled in an attempt to obtain a greater ultimate recovery of oil.

Upon discovery of large enough reserves for commercial drilling, the concept of well spacing becomes important to the oil engineer. The characteristics of reservoirs largely control the well-spacing pattern. For example, reservoirs with thick or multiple zones of oil will usually require more wells, and possibly closer spacing between wells, to take advantage of natural drainage (gravity flow) at its maximum than those reservoirs with thin crude oil composition located in single zones. Furthermore, porous reservoirs will produce more barrels of oil than "tight" reservoirs.

Other factors of a technical nature which should be considered in the spacing of wells, besides thickness versus thinness of the crude itself and the multiple zones versus single zones, include depth to the productive zones of the oil, viscosity of the oil, gravity of the oil, reservoir pressures, and reservoir properties. Therefore, in well spacing, economics of anticipated recoveries based on thickness of oil and saturation of the pay zone become important. Obviously, the greater the number of wells drilled in a single reservoir, the greater will be the ultimate recovery per surface area of oil or gas.

There is a practical limit to the number of wells, and hence the spacing of wells, that can be drilled, however, which is controlled by the cost of drilling and operation. This limit to the number of wells to be drilled is based on estimated ultimate recovery, in barrels of oil, from each well. Since depth is the principal factor governing drilling costs, depth has a bearing on the problem of well spacing.

There is no hard and fast rule on spacing of wells; the technical and nontechnical factors relative to the oil reservoir must be considered separately. Oil wells drilled in the United States are widely spaced and located at the centers of 40-acre tracts or at like ends of 80-acre tracts. For gas wells, on the other hand, spacing ranges between 160 and 640 acres per well. The acreage assigned to each development well is known as a *drilling unit* prior to completion of the well and as a *production unit* upon successful completion.

Usually, the greater the depth to reach productive zones of oil, the wider the spacing of wells. Since viscous oils do not possess the mobility of ready passage through reservoirs, as lighter, less viscous oils do, closer spacing of wells is usually needed with oils of heavy viscosity properties in order to effect maximum efficient drainage. In the case of gravity, the lighter-gravity oils (with the higher API) contain more dissolved gases, have more mobility, and are less viscous than the lower-gravity oils, and so will require fewer wells and wider spacing to effect maximum efficient drainage. Reservoirs with high pressures, particularly if pressures are maintained by some recycling operations such as use of water, gas, or air, offer higher recovery per well. Thus, wider spacing can be employed in reservoirs with high pressures.

Such reservoir properties as porosity, the ability to contain fluids, and permeability influence well spacing. Porous and permeable reservoirs that allow fluids such as oil to flow through the reservoir to the well bore, mean that reservoirs can be effectively drained, so fewer wells with wide spacing are suitable under such conditions. Closer spacing of wells is necessary when "tight" reservoirs, with low porosity and permeability, are involved.

Some nontechnical factors also affect well spacing. These include, for instance, the rate of production desired because of terms of the oil lease, market price of crude, market demand, etc. Also, proration laws of a government can dictate the amount of oil or gas an oil company can produce. When this is the case, the number of wells drilled and the spacing may be affected. Where the rate of payout desired is lengthened and deferment of income over a wide period because of income tax problems is the objective, the number of wells drilled may be cut back. Thus, spacing will tend to be wider under such conditions. Conversely, where the rate of payout desired is for a short period, more wells should be drilled with closer spacing. [1]

---

[1]Hussein K. Abdel-Aal, Mohammed A. Alsahlawi: Petroleum Economics and Engineering. Third Edition. Taylor & Francis Group, LLC. 2014. P 233:234

8. Peak Oil: How Long Can We Depend on Oil and Other Fossil Fuels?

So, when will world oil extraction peak and begin it exorable decline? The peak of oil extraction is reached when approximately half the total has been taken, termed the midpoint of depletion. The determination of a peak is dependent on the total amount of oil that can be extracted from different sources. We obtain this information from estimates of "oil reserves" that include the amount of oil geologists feel can be economically extracted from fields that have been discovered, drilled, and mapped. Many published estimates of world oil reserves have been made since 1942. They have ranged from 600 billion to 3896 billion barrels.

According to Oil & Gas Journal's annual Worldwide Production report, 2012 global oil reserves are 1.6 trillion barrels, up to 115 billion barrels from the number published in 2011.

Overall, ultimate recovery estimates are continually being revised upwards or downwards as new data from exploratory drilling and 3-D seismic surveys become available. For example, the US Geological Survey (USGS) revised its estimate of conventional, undiscovered oil in the National Petroleum Reserve in Alaska from 10.6 billion barrels in 2002 to 896 million barrels in 2010, a 90 % reduction!

The largest estimate of world oil ultimate recovery was made by the USGS in 2000.

The USGS 95 % probable value is 2248 billion barrels. Similarly, the USGS says

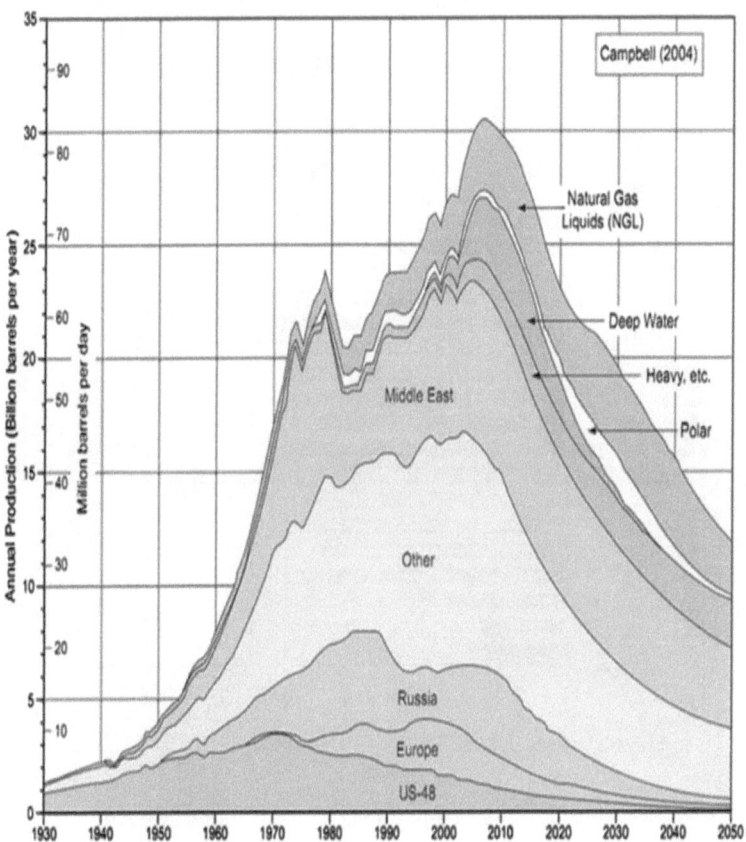

there is a 5 % probability that the value will exceed 3896 billion barrels. The USGS mean estimate (the expected value) is 3003 billion barrels. There are a number of basins, especially in the Arctic and Antarctica, that were not included in the USGS world resource assessment; because, they were judged unlikely to add proved reserves during the next 30 years.

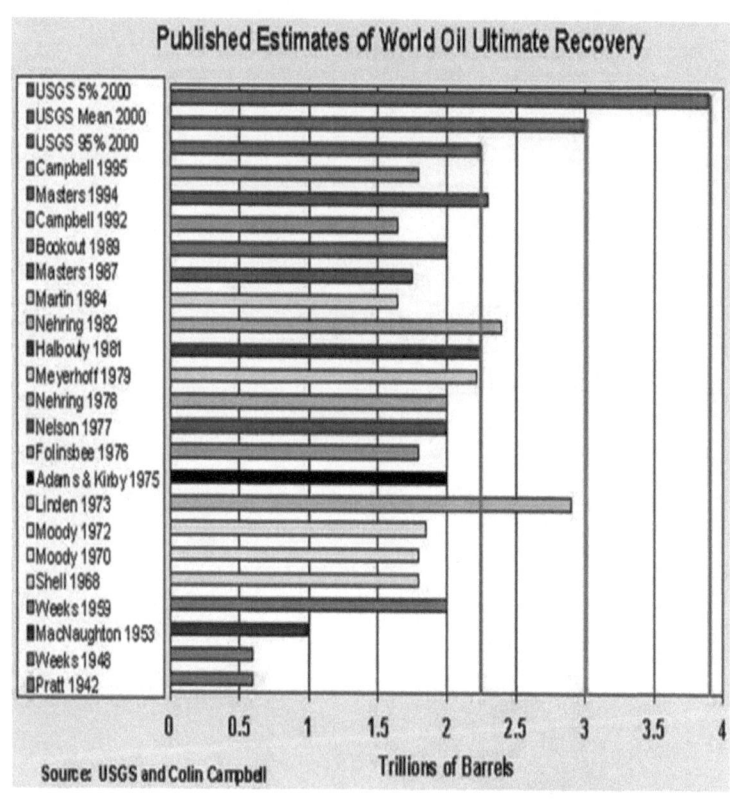

Estimating reserves is problematic, as many country estimates of oil reserves are unreliable or downright exaggerations done for political or economic reasons and are always on the high side. For example, in the 1980s, OPEC changed its oil production quota for its member states to reflect reserves claimed by each. If a member state had higher reserves than other members, it could produce more oil. Surprisingly, there were dramatic increases in reported reserves among OPEC members, but no details were reported on why reserve estimates increased so greatly.

For example, Saudi Arabia in 1988 raised its proved reserves by 50 % and Iran in 2001–2002 by 30 %. Since few new fields were being added, these revisions could not be due to new finds. Calculations of how much oil remains in the ground to be recovered are based on these reserve estimates. If these are in error, it becomes nearly impossible to determine when extraction will go into decline. The OPEC also has a vested economic interest in making the world believe that it sits on immense oil reserves, because to think otherwise might motivate countries to reduce their oil imports through energy efficiency and conservation and by developing alternative sources of energy. They are asking oil importers to "trust us." "Trust, but verify" should be the modus operandi, but for a variety of reasons, including self-interest and fear of losing lucrative markets, their claims of proved reserves have gone unchallenged by oil importers.

So far, we have extracted and used about 1.2 trillion barrels of oil worldwide; the Association for the Study of Peak Oil and Gas (ASPO), USA, estimates that about 1.27 trillion barrels remain, including crude oil, condensate, and NGL (but excluding heavy oil, oil shales, and Canadian tar sands; http://www.aspousa.org/index.php/peak-oil-reference/peak-oil-data/oil-reserves/, accessed 7 December 2010). Since 1972, there have been dozens of different estimates of the year of Peak Oil, ranging from earlier predictions of 1996 (M. King Hubbert in 1977) to no visible peak likely. Based on the USGS mean estimate of 3 trillion barrels, the US Energy Information Agency (EIA) estimated that Peak Oil would not occur until 2037. Others have placed global oil reserves at 2–2.5 trillion barrels, implying that the peak is much closer. Many oil fields, countries, and oil companies have already peaked. Sixty-four of 100 + oil-producing countries are in decline, including Norway, Venezuela, UK, Indonesia, etc.; and individual companies have also peaked, including Chevron, Exxon, Shell, and Total. Certain grades, for example, light sweet crude, have also peaked. The most recent ASPO model suggests that worldwide "conventional" oil peaked in 2005 and "conventional plus nonconventional" oil peaked in 2008 (revised 3 October 2009; http://aspoireland.

files.wordpress.com/2009/12/newsletter100_200904.pdf, accessed 7 December 2010. Further evidence that oil production has reached a maximum comes from the US DOE. In March 2010, it admitted that "a chance exists that we may experience a decline" of world liquid fuels production between 2011 and 2015 "if the investment is not there". In March 2010, using an updated version of the Hubbert model, Kuwaiti scientists predicted that global oil production will peak in 2014. They included many Hubbert production cycles reflecting the influence of new technological innovations, government regulations, economic conditions, and political events. In spite of differences in the timing of Peak Oil, all agree on the fact that oil is a finite and very valuable resource. [1]

Predicting peak conventional oil production for the world is different to predicting peak in a region. If a given region peaks, the world's supply of oil can be met by production ramping up in other regions, as has happened many times in the past; most notably when US Lower-48 conventional oil production peaked in 1970, with enough production to more than compensate coming from new, but already-discovered, regions such as Alaska, the North

---

[1]J. Edward Gates • David L. Trauger • Brian Czech: Peak Oil, Economic Growth, and Wildlife Conservation. Springer Science+Business Media New York 2014. P 17: 21

Sea, and in Mexico, Russia and elsewhere. To understand the global peak of conventional oil two new factors need to be considered: the comparative cost of conventional oil production from different regions and for different classes of oil, and also the global price of oil.

The comparative costs are needed because as one region or class of oil goes into decline (or is restricted into the market for political or other reasons), conventional oil from other regions or classes may replace it; the price of oil needs to be known to see if this is high enough to support such marginal production. [1]

It does not matter what the EROI of a fuel is if it is depleted. So, we first examine the issue of how much fossil fuels we are likely to have. The best-known model of oil production was developed by Marion King Hubbert, who proposed that the discovery and production of petroleum over time would first grow exponentially and then reach a peak when roughly half the resource had been exploited, followed by a more or less symmetrical decline; that is the production of oil for a region, a country or the world would follow a more or less symmetric, bell-shaped curve. He surmised that the rate of production would initially increase

[1] R.W. Bentley: Introduction to Peak Oil. Springer International Publishing Switzerland 2016. P 45

exponentially as the means for exploiting and using the resource were figured out. A peak in production would occur when about 50 % of the ultimate recoverable resources (URR) had been extracted (he later opined that there may be more than one peak). URR is the total amount of oil that can be recovered. Hubbert's hypothesis was based principally on his experience as a geologist and it was not a bad guess. He famously predicted in 1956 that US oil production from the lower 48 states would peak in 1970, which in fact it did. Hubbert also predicted that the US production of natural gas would peak in about 1980, which it did, although it has since shown signs of recovery and there is a second peak in early 2015 based on large part on "unconventional" and "shale gas." He also predicted that world oil production would peak in about 2000. In fact, the production of oil globally continued to increase until 2005, after which it appears to have entered an "undulating plateau," as predicted earlier by geologists Campbell and Laherrere. The main reason that the Hubbert Curve "works" is that if the finding of oil peaks at some point then inevitably and due to the simplest of math (the integral of the production curve cannot exceed the integral of the finding curve) the peak of production must follow. For the United States the peak in finding oil was in the 1930s and for the world in the 1960s. Both have declined enormously since then and production declines must follow.

In the past several decades, a number of 'neo-Hubbertarians' have made predictions about the timing of global and national oil production peaks using several variations of Hubbert's approach. Various forecasts of the timing of global peak have ranged from one predicted for 1989 to many predicted for the first decade of the Twenty-first century to one as late as 2040. The difference in these forecasts is largely due to differences in assumptions about the URR (ultimate recoverable resource). Brandt (2007), Nashawi et al. (2010) and Hallock et al. (2014) show that the Hubbert Curve is a good predictor for most post-peak nations, which includes the majority of all oil-producing nations. Other forecasts for world oil production do not rely on such curve-fitting techniques to make future projections and/or a prior assumption about URR. According to one forecast by the US Energy Information Agency (EIA 2003), world oil supply in 2025 will exceed the 2001 level by 53 %. [1]

The EIA reviewed five other world oil models and found that all of them predict that production will increase over the next two decades to around 100 million barrels per day, substantially more than the 80 million barrels per day produced in 2016 (The production of "all liquids", which includes conventional crude

---

[1] Charles A.S. Hall: Energy Return on Investment. 2017. P 146: 147

oil plus fracked oil, natural gas liquids, biofuels, refinery gains and so on, was 96 million barrels per day). Several of these models rely on the 2000 USGS estimates of URR for oil. Thus, it does seem that the production of "conventional oil" is at a rough plateau, but that other materials such as natural gas liquids and shale oil are still increasing. At a minimum, the annual rate of increase in global oil production has fallen from about 5 % to less than 1 %. [1]

How long can the oil supply satisfy the oil demand? This question depends on at least three factors. The first factor concerns the total amount of the resource which is found and can be extracted. Apart from the obvious fact that the quantity has to be finite, there is no exact public knowledge of how large our remaining petroleum resources exactly are. In addition, the constant ongoing search for oil results in a almost continuous discovery of new oil fields. The present discovery rate is about 10 Gb (Giga barrels or 109 oil barrels) per year, which is significantly lower than the annual consumption of about 30 Gb.

A common term in the industry is to consider "2P" reserves as the best estimate for the remaining commercial resource base for conventional oil. 2P means the already proven

---

[1]Charles A.S. Hall: Energy Return on Investment. 2017. P 147

reserves and the unproven reserves which are "likely" to be found with a probability larger than 50 %. The global world estimate of the 2P reserve has been evaluated to be about 1,000Gb. The uncertainty is about±300Gb.Up till now (2013), humans have already used about 1,100 Gb (Aleklett et al. 2012) which shows that as compared to a bottle of Coke, we have now most likely emptied more than half of it. Also, compared to the present annual consumption of oil we see that the resource is emptied in about 30 years from now if the production is kept constant. [1]

In addition to the uncertainty in the resource base there are other factors which affect our estimate. The first is increased demand, through population growth and increased industrialization of large countries like India and China. A second problem is related two what today is known as the Hubbert "Peak Oil Theory" (Hubbert 1956). It says that the production from a finite resource can only increase for a limited time until a maximum production is achieved. This time is called "Peak oil", *tpeak* . After "Peak Oil" the production will decline no matter how much the demand would be—unless revolutionary new production technologies are discovered. The only way to

---

[1]Patrick A. Narbel • Jan Petter Hansen Jan R. Lien: Energy Technologies and Economics. Springer International Publishing Switzerland 2014. P 103

meet an increased demand after peak oil for a given resource is to find additional resources. Regarding conventional oil this is at present more unlikely than likely: Almost half of the oil resources exist in so-called giant oil fields which were discovered more than 50 years ago. Continuous search in increasingly more harsh environments (arctics, deep oceans) have so far not changed the almost constant and slowly decaying curve of new discoveries. In 2011 three new Norwegian oil fields were found in the North Sea and in the Barents Sea which were reported as significant and large. However, the estimated total amount of oil within these fields will only be able to cover the present global oil consumption for about a month! [1]

8.1. Economic Impacts of Peak Oil and Decreasing EROI

In the past few decades, many petroleum geologists have become convinced that global output of petroleum (and of natural gas soon after) is about to peak or may have peaked already. From the perspective of 2016 it appears that production of oil from "conventional" sources—so to speak—may indeed have peaked, although there is still some oil to be found in deep water (e.g. off the coast of Brazil), in very remote places (e.g. the

[1] Patrick A. Narbel • Jan Petter Hansen Jan R. Lien: Energy Technologies and Economics. Springer International Publishing Switzerland 2014. P 104

Arctic), or in tar sands and shale. Unconventional oil is much more expensive to find and recover than oil from the Middle East, but with new technology it is still profitable at high enough prices. Investment in unconventional oil depends on prices.

This geological scarcity, together with rising demand from China and India, and turmoil in the Middle East, seemed to be reflected in pre-2014 prices. But short-term oil price movements have several drivers, including futures speculation, OPEC politics, the Sunni-Shia rivalry in Islam, Russian and Iranian affairs, the slowing of the Chinese economy and declining US demand for gas guzzlers. Notwithstanding the turmoil, an upward long-term price trend, seems sure to follow eventually. The deeper the bottom the faster (and higher) the price recovery is likely to be. Geology does drive the recovery price of oil in the longer term.

The fact that discoveries have lagged behind consumption has been known for a long time. The reality of peak oil has been obscured up to now by sudden but unexplained increases in officially reported reserves in the Middle East in the late 1980s, and uncritical forecasts by industry figures and government agencies. These optimistic forecasts are strongly influenced by mainstream economists who still argue—as they did in their response to the "Limits to Growth" book (Meadows et al. 1972)—that there is still plenty of oil in the ground and that rising prices will automatically trigger more discovery and more efficient methods of recovery.

Discovery of conventional oil peaked in the US in 1930 and globally in 1965. Total discoveries in a given year have not kept up with depletion since 1982 (except for 1992) and the ratio of discovery to depletion is continuously declining. An influential oil consultancy, Wood-MacKenzie, noted in 2004 that oil companies were discovering an average of 20 million bbl/day, while global consumption was up to 75 million bbl/day. The discrepancy is even worse now that daily global consumption is around 95 million bbl. [1]

So-called 'proved resources' (90% certain) were still increasing (barely) a few years ago because formerly 'proved and probable' resources (50% certain) are being converted to 'proved' as existing fields are fully explored. But the latter category is the one that best predicts future supplies—and the two curves are converging. Big publicly traded oil companies are showing increased reserves, but what they do not mention is that this appearance of growth is mostly from "drilling on Wall Street"—i.e.

---

[1] Robert Ayres: ENERGY, COMPLEXITY AND WEALTH MAXIMIZATION. Springer International Publishing Switzerland 2016. P 305

buying existing smaller companies—rather than drilling in the earth. Because share values supposedly reflect reserves, companies that did not adopt this strategy—like Shell—faced strong pressures a few years ago to meddle with their reserve statistics in order to reassure stockholders.

Now Shell seems to have switched to the acquisition strategy. On-shore production, before shale, peaked in the 1970s. Combined on-shore and off-shore production peaked in 2005. 'Gas liquids', which are an indication of aging, are the only category still increasing. US production peaked in 1969–1970, just before Prudhoe Bay came on stream, and even that discovery did not raise US output above the 1970 level. The Cantarell field in Mexico, the second largest ever found, is well beyond its peak and output is declining fast. North Sea output has peaked and is now declining. The giant Kashagan field, discovered in 2000 (with an estimated 13 billion barrels of recoverable, but high sulfur, oil) is under the northern part of the Caspian Sea. It has been called "the last pearl in the crown of the world oil industry". Kashagan is now under development by a consortium of companies but has proved to be very complex and expensive ($135 billion spent so far), and harmful to wildlife. Commercial production only started in 2013 (full production expected in 2017). The oil will be going to China via a new pipeline.

In 2007 the Brazilian nationalized company Petrobras announced the discovery of a 5 billion barrel "giant" field off the coast south of Rio de Janeiro. It may presage a larger ("super-giant") field in the Santos Basin with up to 50 billion barrels of recoverable oil. However, it is located under dense layers of salt at a depth of 10 km below the ocean surface, so getting the oil out will not be easy. The energy return on energy invested (EROI) is unlikely to be better than 10 (typical of deep water fields) which means that 5 billion of the 50 billion barrels of possible output will be used—as exergy—for the recovery, refining and distribution. Corruption in Petrobras has destabilized the Brazilian government. Russian output looks like it will peak very soon if it has not done so already. The director of one of the largest Russian firms says that his country will never produce more than 10 Mb/d. The CEO of Total (the French oil major) has said that 100 Mb/d is the absolute maximum for world production. According to the British Petroleum (BP) Statistical Review, of 54 producing nations only 14 still show increasing production, 30 are past peak output, while output rates are declining in 10. [1]

---

[1] Robert Ayres: ENERGY, COMPLEXITY AND WEALTH MAXIMIZATION. Springer International Publishing Switzerland 2016. P 308: 309

Most non-OPEC oil producing countries (except the US) are now in decline, and very few significant countries, mostly in the Middle East, claim to be able to increase output. The "end of oil" may not be an immediate threat (thanks to other factors). But the halfway point, corresponding to peak output, is likely to be just around the corner, i.e. probably 5–15 years in the future.

But as the discovery rate has slowed, the energy and other costs of replacing oil that has already been consumed are now rising fast. The energy return on energy invested (EROI) of oil discovered in the 1930s and 1940s was about 110, but for the oil produced in the 1970s it has been estimated as 23, while for new oil discovered in that decade it was only 8. This was still tolerable since only 12% of the oil discovered was needed to discover, drill, refine and distribute it. In the case of deep-water oil, and for heavy oil, the EROI is currently estimated to be about 10.

The end of near total dependence on fossil fuels is already in sight, although a little more distant than was thought a decade ago. Some years ago the oil geologist M. King Hubbert, taking into account discovery rates and depletion rates of known fields, predicted that global oil output would peak between 2000 and 2010. Others, notably Colin Campbell and Jean Laherre`re came to the same conclusion

(Campbell and Laherre`re 1998). From the perspective of nine years later (2014) it can be seen that global oil production did not actually peak in the period 2005–2013. Data from EIA for 2003 through 2015 show clearly that production from standard "legacy" sources of crude oil, such as the OPEC countries, Africa and Russia, did not increase. The small increase in total output since 2005 has been entirely due to US shale oil and Canadian tar sands production, known as "unconventional" oil.

However, whereas a number of influential reports in the 2009–2019 era predicted a gap by 2015 of up to ten million bbl/day between demand and supply, the opposite situation actually occurred. The ten million bbl/day gap has become a two million bbl/day glut.

It is worthwhile to look at oil prices over time. The two dramatic "spikes" in 1979, 1979–1980 and 2008 (and a small one in 1991) have all been followed by recessions (indicated by the gray shade.). The question causing such volatility in the stock-market in the winter of 2016, was mostly whether the current low oil price will cause another recession, despite the (fairly) strong US economic data.

Evidently a small change in output after 2008 was followed by a very large change in price, although the indirect effects on the global economy, resulting in sharply reduced global demand, were mainly responsible. But when the economic downturn "bottomed" in 2009, the price went up again and stayed fairly high for several years. The price peaked over $100/bbl in 2011 and remained near or above $90/bbl until midsummer 2014. John Watson, CEO of Chevron, has said in interviews during that period that $100/bbl is "the new reality" in the crude oil business and that "costs have caught up to revenues for many classes of projects." In 2013 or so it was being said around the executive suites that $100/bbl had reached OPEC's "threshold of pain". This is because many oil-producing countries were, even then, earning less from petroleum sales than their national budgetary requirements. [1]

It is well known that there is a strong correlation between a nation's, and the world's, energy use and material well-being. There also is a strong correlation between a nation's total energy use, its EROI and the equity of its distribution, and both GDP and more importantly various indices of human well-being, such as the HDI (human development index), at least up to some point. If we are to maintain or increase human well-being into a future of possible decreasing energy availability,

---

[1] Robert Ayres: ENERGY, COMPLEXITY AND WEALTH MAXIMIZATION. Springer International Publishing Switzerland 2016. P 310: 312

we will have to think very carefully about how to do so. A more equitable distribution of energy resources is one logical place to start.

Whether global peak oil has occurred already, or will not occur for some years or, conceivably, decades, its economic implications will be enormous. Hamilton (2009) has found that all economic recessions in recent decades in the United States had been preceded by an increase in the price of oil. As oil becomes less readily available in future decades, we do not know if there are substitutes available on the scale required and at the EROI that is needed.

Alternatives will require enormous investments in money and energy, both likely to be in short supply. Despite the projected impact on our economic and business life within relatively few years in the USA, neither government nor the business community is prepared to deal with either the impacts of these changes or the new thinking needed for investment strategies (Hall and Klitgaard 2012; Hirsch et al. 2005; Hall and Groat 2010). The reasons are myriad but include: the vested interests of powerful energy companies, the disinterest and disorientation of the media, the erosion of good energy record keeping at the Department of Commerce, and the focus of the media on trivial "silver bullets" despite the inability of any one of them (except economic contraction and in some cases conservation) to contribute more than a few percent to the total energy mix, and the failure of government to fund good objective analytic work on the various energy options. Consequently, much of what is written about energy is woefully misinformed or simply advocacy by various groups that hope to look good or profit from various perceived alternatives.

The end of cheap petroleum will be perhaps the most important challenge that Western society has ever faced, especially when considered within the context of the need to deal with climate change, growing populations, and aspirations and other environmental issues related to energy (Jones and Warner 2016). Business and government leaders who do not understand the inevitability, seriousness, and implications of the end of cheap oil and eventually cheap fossil fuels, or who make poor decisions in an attempt to alleviate their impact, are likely to be tremendously and negatively affected as a result. At the same time the investment decisions made in the next decades will determine whether or not civilization is to make it through the transition away from petroleum driven, growth-based economies to something more sustainable, if indeed that is possible. [1]

---

[1] Charles A.S. Hall: Energy Return on Investment. 2017. P 155: 159

It must also be considered that at current production rates US gas reserves (both conventional and unconventional) will be exhausted in 14 years, while other major gas producers can rely on longer periods of production: 70 years for Russia and over 200 years for Qatar and Iran, which together represent 30 % of the world supply of natural gas. At the same time, it is worth recalling that a decade ago, when shale reserves were still not exploited, the predicted years of future US production were definitely less than today. Similarly, oil reserves are projected to last for another 11 years, which compares with a world average of 55. In spite of this, every year the amount of new reserves discovered is at least equal to the annual production, leaving the years of potential future supply unchanged. [1]

---

[1] Rossella Bardazzi • Maria Grazia Pazienza Alberto Tonini: European Energy and Climate Security. Springer International Publishing Switzerland 2016. P 136

9. Oil reservoirs in some countries
9.1. Nigeria

Nigeria is a leading oil and gas (OG) producer in Africa and an important supplier to the international energy market. Of the 58.4% of oil imported into the US for consumption in June 2001, 3.9% (765,000 bod) came from Nigeria. In 2001, Nigeria ranked fifth in supplying crude oil to the US—after Canada, Saudi Arabia, Venezuela, and Mexico (Boston Globe 2001). Nigeria leads Africa's six top OG nations, followed by Libya, Algeria, Angola, Sudan, and Egypt. [1]

Nigeria and other African producers of OG are growing in significance in world energy markets as a result of the combination of many factors. China and India, until their recent economic slowdowns, were consuming large quantities of crude petroleum because of rapid industrial expansion and growing energy needs. By 2014, for instance, China had become the second-largest economy behind the US after economic growth rates of almost 10% in 2010 to slightly above 6% in 2015 (Magnier 2016). There is also the fact that especially in the US, while existing nuclear plants were getting old and placed out of commission, fewer ones are being built due to safety concerns (Ernest and

---

[1] Kwamina Panford: Africa's Natural Resources and Underdevelopment. 2017. P 53

Young 2013). Besides, due to a preference for clean energy, natural gas in the form of liquid petroleum gas (LPG) is becoming fundamental to economic growth as a source of power for both domestic and industrial use. So natural gas is becoming a significant contributor to industrial take-off and development generally. For rail and road transport, natural gas is becoming a crucial ingredient for attaining higher efficiency and clean-burning fuel. Gas burns 80% more efficiently than petrol. Hence the Boston-area, Massachusetts Bay Transport Authority's buses now run on compressed natural gas (CNG) to save money and the environment. Increasingly, commercial vehicles, mostly taxis and small buses in major Ghanaian cities, use propane gas, a derivative of natural gas, because it is more efficient than regular gas (as it called in the US) or petrol in Africa. [1]

Nigeria is not only a major petroleum state in Africa; it is also one of the first, if not the first, to discover and produce petroleum in commercial quantities. Crude OG were first found in 1956 at Oloibiri, Niger Delta by Shell-BP. By then Shell-BP was the only company allowed by the British colonial authorities to explore for oil in Nigeria. In 1958 (two years before independence), Nigeria exported its first crude of 5,100 barrels of oil daily (bod) to the

---

[1]Kwamina Panford: Africa's Natural Resources and Underdevelopment. 2017. P 53: 54

international market. Currently, Libya with 46,420 billion barrels of oil (bbo) has Africa's largest reserve of crude and ranks 9th in the world. Nigeria is second in Africa with 36.2 bbo and is number 10 in the world. Nigeria, however, is number 1 in terms of oil exports. In the last decade, Nigeria's output and exports range from 2m to 2.5m barrels daily followed by the number two producer, Angola with approximately 1.8, barrels each day. [1]

9.2. Angola

The socio-economic profile of Angola is that of a resource-rich but a severely underdeveloped country. It is a classic petro-state despite its diamonds. Oil and gas account for 60% of the economy; 80% of government incomes and as high as 97% of incomes come from OG exports. Its spectacular wealth in diamonds is confirmed by a recent discovery. This diamond, the size of a tennis ball and the largest diamond found in more than a century, was appraised in New York City by Sotheby's Auction on 3 May 2016 at $70 million. [2]

Angola ranked 10th as a provider of crude oil to the US in 2001. It produced slightly below 2 million bods and exported 283,000 bods to the US in 2001, constituting 1.4% of US

([1])Kwamina Panford: Africa's Natural Resources and Underdevelopment. 2017. P 54
([2])Kwamina Panford: Africa's Natural Resources and Underdevelopment. 2017. P 61

consumption in 2001 (*Boston Globe* 2001). Currently, Angola is second to Nigeria as Africa's leading OG nation. In 2012, its output was 1.8 bod and in 2012 it supplied 2.9% of US oil needs. Besides, Angola is also a major crude supplier to China.

It provided for China 16% of its requirements in July 2012 (Mendes and McClelland 2012). Angola has the fourth-largest proven oil reserves on the African continent after Libya, Nigeria, and Algeria in that order. Angola has 9.5 billion barrels in proven reserves (AU 2013, 89). At its rate of output, Angola supplied 1.6% of the global oil market's needs (Wall Street Journal 2007). It was also a top-tier natural gas producer at number 5 in Africa with 10,947 tcf in 2012. [1]

Several factors explain Angola's utter failure to convert its enormous wealth, including its fabulous gem diamonds, into improved quality of life for most of its population. Foremost is a 27-year civil war. The war started before independence (11 November 1975) and lasted until February 2002 when Jonas Savimbi, the rebel leader of the Union for the Total Liberation of Angola (UNITA), was killed (New African 2002). Second, Angola's proximity to Zaire and also its geographical location as a

---

[1] Kwamina Panford: Africa's Natural Resources and Underdevelopment. 2017. P 62

frontline state in the Southern African region close to the white minority regime in South Africa, which entangled it in a complex web of East–West Cold War ideological battles inflamed by commercial and geostrategic interests in diamond, oil and gas is well captured by New African. [1]

Equatorial Guinea: A Small Petroleum-Rich but not Socially Prosperous Country Like Angola and the Democratic Republic of Congo (DR Congo), Equatorial Guinea is rich in crude petroleum And yet it is one of the least developed nations and among the most politically repressive in the world. According to the government, in 2012 it supplied 17% of all the gas consumed for heating, cooling, cooking and other domestic and industrial uses in the US (New York Times 28 December 2012, A7). With an estimated reserve of 1.1 billion barrels, it has Africa's 10th and the world's 39th biggest crude reserves. It also has current and future potentials to remain one of Africa's leading natural gas producers (AU 2013, 89). The country poses an interesting riddle: It has a small population, 820,885 people in 2014 (Equatorial Guinea, EIU, 1st Quarter Report 2016), but a relatively large output of both oil (250,200 bod) and natural gas, thus having a high per capita income of $12,476 in

---

[1]Kwamina Panford: Africa's Natural Resources and Underdevelopment. 2017. P 62

2011. Between 2000 and 2011, the per capita income shot up 272%.

Despite its middle-income type of income, like its resource-rich neighbor, Angola, Equatorial Guinea displays all the hallmarks of a resource-rich, but development-poor or deprived nation. It is both one of the most politically repressed and least economically advanced in Africa. The Africa Progress Panel (2013) cites it as one of the "well-being deficit resource-rich countries" in the world. With Gabon (another oil rich, but poor country) and Nigeria, Equatorial Guinea exhibits low levels of primary school attendance and high gender inequality in education. It lags behind many countries with less resources such as Poland and Vietnam in critical human development areas: Life expectancy was 51 years in 2011; the level of under-5 mortality was 118 per 1000 and maternal mortality was 240 per 100,000 live births in 2010. The poor state of the nation's health services is depicted by the fact that 24 out of 10,000 women who give birth die in Equatorial Guinea. [1]

9.3. Ghana

Oil and gas (OG) exploration preceded independence and the 2007 Jubilee Field oil find in Ghana. Earlier, small quantities of crude oil

---

[1] Kwamina Panford: Africa's Natural Resources and Underdevelopment. 2017. P 68: 69

were produced offshore near Saltpond. The first petroleum activities occurred in the 1880s in the Tano Basin which coincided with the introduction of commercial gold mining and cocoa production (Panford 2012, 2014a, b; Asafu-Adjaye 2012). The Tano Basin Exploration did not yield much oil as only a few barrels were produced. Then in 1970, an Amoco-led consortium found oil offshore Saltpond. This field was developed by Agripetco and produced initially, 400 barrels of oil daily (bod). Declining production caused a shutdown in 1984 (Asafo-Adjei 2012). When petroleum prices rose and technology improved, in 2000, GNPC (Ghana's national oil company (NOC)) and Lushann Internit revived production. As of 2012, the Salt pond field produced 700 bods.

There was an important oil activity besides the Saltpond oil field. Less than 20 miles from the Jubilee Field, in the South Tano area, in the 1970s, Phillips Petroleum discovered oil and a test well produced 62,000 barrels of oil (Asafo-Adjei 2012, 13). The Soviets were also involved in petroleum exploration in Ghana. Prior to the coup of 1966 in which Kwame Nkrumah and the Convention People's Party (CPP) were toppled, Russians explored oil on shore in the Volta Basin. The Soviets left Ghana with the oil data they had accumulated when the military junta kicked them out of Ghana.

Currently, a few Russian companies, including Lukoil, are involved in mostly downstream oil activities—the retail of oil products such as petrol (gasoline), engine oil as well as other lubricants.

Since May 2015, the Russians have discussed with the GoG their plans to enhance their involvement in upstream oil activities through partnerships exploring for oil in the Deepwater Tano Project area in Ghana. The Chinese have also participated in Ghana's infant OG sector. Through a Chinese government loan of $1 billion, China's SINOPEC was the lead contractor that built the gas infrastructure to transport natural gas from the floating production storage and offloading (FPSO) Kwame Nkrumah MV21 at the Jubilee Field to Atuabo in the Ellembelle District (Western Region) for processing. This Chinese funded construction project is crucial to Ghana's efforts to monetize the gas produced at Jubilee which is estimated to be worth between $1 billion and – $2 billion. [1]

9.4. china

Statistics show a clear decline in China's proven and recoverable petroleum reserves. In 1987 there were 2,377 mmt declining to 2,322 mmt by the end of 1997 and

---

[1]Kwamina Panford: Africa's Natural Resources and Underdevelopment. 2017. P 91: 92

2,117 mmt by 2008. Chinese petroleum reserves presently account for 1.3% of the world total (BP 2008). As of the end 2007, the ratio of reserves to production was 11.3 years. Finding new oil fields and creating a comprehensive oil import policy package is one of the most important tasks for China to undertake. Similarly, oil reserves are not evenly distributed over Provinces, which shows stocks in favor of Northeast (Heilongjiang), East (Jiangsu) and Northwest (Xinjiang). [1]

China's proven reserves of natural gas are 1.9 trillion cubic meters and account for 1.1% of the world total. As of the end 2007, the ratio of reserves to production is 27.2. Natural gas reserves are mainly located in the Southwest (Sichuan and Chongqing), West (Shaanxi), North (Inner Mongolia) and Northwest (Xinjiang). There are two types of natural gas reserves – those which are independent of oil fields and those associated with oil reserves. Natural gas development is sluggish due to the absence of production facilities, transportation pipelines and urban gas supply systems. Nevertheless, China's natural gas resources are estimated to be large and more will no doubt be confirmed and developed. The most promising fields are in the Ordos basin, the Caidam Basin, and the Yinggehai Basin off Hainan Island. [2]

---

[1]Hengyun Ma l Les Oxley: China's Energy Economy. Springer-Verlag Berlin Heidelberg 2012. P 52: 53

References

1. Charles A.S. Hall: Energy Return on Investment. 2017.
2. Congrui Jin • Gianluca Cusatis: New Frontiers in Oil and Gas Exploration. Springer International Publishing Switzerland 2016.
3. Cyrus Bina: A Prelude to the Foundation of Political Economy. PALGRAVE MACMILLAN. 2013.
4. Ehsan Khamehchi • Mohammad Reza Mahdiani: Gas Allocation Optimization Methods in Artificial Gas Lift. 2017.
5. Fadi Henri Nader: Multi-scale Quantitative Diagenesis and Impacts on Heterogeneity of Carbonate Reservoir Rocks. Springer International Publishing AG 2017.
6. Frank Jahn, Mark Cook and Mark Graham: HYDROCARBON EXPLORATION AND PRODUCTION. 2ND EDITION. Elsevier B.V. 2008.
7. Hengyun Ma I Les Oxley: China's Energy Economy. Springer-Verlag Berlin Heidelberg 2012.
8. http://www.opec.org/opec_web/en/index.htm
9. Hussein K. Abdel-Aal Mohamed A. Aggour Mohamed A. Fahim: Petroleum and Gas Field Processing. Second Edition. Taylor & Francis Group, LLC. 2016.

(^{2})Hengyun Ma l Les Oxley: China's Energy Economy. Springer-Verlag Berlin Heidelberg 2012. P 53: 54

10. Hussein K. Abdel-Aal, Mohammed A. Alsahlawi: Petroleum Economics and Engineering. Third Edition. Taylor & Francis Group, LLC. 2014.
11. Iakovos Alhadeff: USA Russia & China in the Middle East. Free ebook.net 2014.
12. J. Edward Gates • David L. Trauger • Brian Czech: Peak Oil, Economic Growth, and Wildlife Conservation. Springer Science+Business Media New York 2014.
13. James G. Speight: The Chemistry and Technology of Petroleum. FOURTH EDITION. Taylor & Francis Group, LLC. 2007.
14. Jinjun Xue • Zhongxiu Zhao • Yande Dai • Bo Wang: Green Low-Carbon Development in China. Springer International Publishing Switzerland 2013.
15. Kirsten Heimann • Obulisamy Parthiba Karthikeyan Subramanian Senthilkannan Muthu: Biodegradation and Bioconversion of Hydrocarbons. Springer Science+Business Media Singapore 2017.
16. Kun Sang Lee • Tae Hong Kim: Integrative Understanding of Shale Gas Reservoirs. 2016.
17. Kwamina Panford: Africa's Natural Resources and Underdevelopment. 2017.
18. MIHIR K. SINHA, LARRY R. PADGETT: RESERVOIR ENGINEERING TECHNIQUES USING FORTRAN. D. Reidel Publishing Company 1985.
19. Nick Bahrami: Evaluating Factors Controlling Damage and Productivity in Tight Gas

Reservoirs. Doctoral Thesis. Springer International Publishing Switzerland 2013.
20. Nuno Luis Madureira: Key Concepts in Energy. Springer International Publishing Switzerland 2014.
21. Patrick A. Narbel • Jan Petter Hansen Jan R. Lien: Energy Technologies and Economics. Springer International Publishing Switzerland 2014.
22. R.W. Bentley: Introduction to Peak Oil. Springer International Publishing Switzerland 2016.
23. Ripudaman Malhotra: Fossil Energy. Springer Science+Business Media New York 2013.
24. Robert Ayres: ENERGY, COMPLEXITY AND WEALTH MAXIMIZATION. Springer International Publishing Switzerland 2016.
25. Roger Boyd: Energy and the Financial System Springer Cham Heidelberg New York Dordrecht London 2013.
26. Rossella Bardazzi • Maria Grazia Pazienza Alberto Tonini: European Energy and Climate Security. Springer International Publishing Switzerland 2016.
27. Sanjib Chowdhury: Optimization and Business Improvement Studies in Upstream Oil and Gas Industry. John Wiley & Sons, Inc. 2016.
28. Sidney Borowitz: FAREWELL FOSSIL FUELS Reviewing America' s. Energy Policy. Plenum Press, New York in 1999.

29. Simone Tagliapietra: Energy Relations in the Euro-Mediterranean. 2017.
30. Stephen J. McPhail • Viviana Cigolotti Angelo Moreno: Fuel Cells in the Waste-to-Energy Chain. Springer-Verlag London Limited 2012.
31. Tayvis Dunnahoe: OGJ Exploration. 2018
32. Uttam Ray Chaudhuri: Fundamentals of Petroleum and Petrochemical Engineering. Taylor and Francis Group. 2011.
33. V. Vishal • T.N. Singh: Geologic Carbon Sequestration. Springer International Publishing Switzerland 2016.
34. World Energy Resources. World Energy Council. 2016.
35. Xuetao Hu • Shuyong Hu Fayang Jin • Su Huang: Physics of petroleum Reservoirs, Petroleum Industry Press, Beijing, China 2017.

Biography of the author

Roshdy Ebrahim Abdin, Egyptian.

Ph.D (economics)

Economics lecturer.

Member at the Egyptian assembly for political economy.

Member at the Egyptian assembly for international law.

Professional diploma in arbitration.

diploma in importing and exporting.

Lawyer since 2008.

For more information please subscribe to my blog:

http://roshdyebrahim.blogspot.com.eg/

the author's books
1. Economic study of Oil and Gas Well Drilling
2. Economic study of Oil and Gas Exploration
3. Economics of oil and gas production
4. Economics of Petroleum, principles
5. Economics of petroleum market
6. Explanatory of petroleum market volatility

www.ingramcontent.com/pod-product-compliance
Lightning Source LLC
Chambersburg PA
CBHW031612210526
45464CB00004B/1538